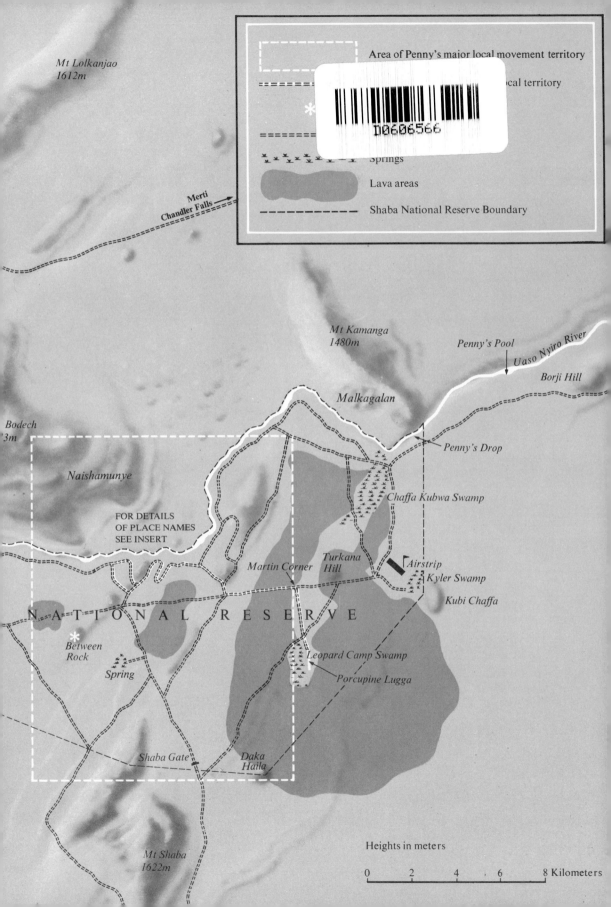

Mt Lolkanjao
1612m

Merti
Chandler Falls

Area of Penny's major local movement territory

D0606566

Springs

Lava areas

Shaba National Reserve Boundary

Mt Kamanga
1480m

Penny's Pool

Uaso Nyiro River

Borji Hill

Malkagalan

Bodech
3m

Penny's Drop

Naishamunye

Chaffa Kubwa Swamp

FOR DETAILS
OF PLACE NAMES
SEE INSERT

Martin Corner

Turkana
Hill

Airstrip

Kyler Swamp

Kubi Chaffa

N A T I O N A L   R E S E R V E

Between
Rock

Leopard Camp Swamp

Spring

Porcupine Lugga

Shaba Gate

Daka
Haila

Mt Shaba
1622m

Heights in meters

0   2   4   6   8 Kilometers

QUEEN OF SHABA

Other books by Joy Adamson

BORN FREE

LIVING FREE

FOREVER FREE

THE SPOTTED SPHINX

PIPPA'S CHALLENGE

THE PEOPLES OF KENYA

JOY ADAMSON'S AFRICA

THE SEARCHING SPIRIT: AN AUTOBIOGRAPHY

JOY ADAMSON

QUEEN OF
SHABA

The Story of an African Leopard

A HELEN AND KURT WOLFF BOOK
HARCOURT BRACE JOVANOVICH
NEW YORK AND LONDON

Requests for permission to make copies of any part of the work should be mailed to: Permissions, Harcourt Brace Jovanovich, Inc., 757 Third Avenue, New York, N.Y. 10017.

Library of Congress Cataloging in Publication Data

Adamson, Joy.
Queen of Shaba.
"A Helen and Kurt Wolff book."
1. Leopards—Legends and stories. 2. Leopards —Behavior. 3. Adamson, Joy. 4. Mammals—Zaire —Shaba. I. Title.
QL795.L5A32   636.8'9   80-7931
ISBN 0-15-175651-1

Printed in the United States of America

First American edition

B C D E

CONTENTS

Illustrations are between pages 54 and 55,
86 and 87, 118 and 119, 150 and 151.

QUEEN OF SHABA

Beginnings

In 1965 when I was camping in Meru National Park studying the behavior of wild cheetahs, I was given a female leopard cub, 4 weeks old. I named her Taga; she was endearing and highly intelligent and stimulated me to plan that when I had completed the rehabilitation of my cheetah Pippa and her four litters, which I calculated would not be till 1970, I would then devote myself to studying leopard behavior. Sadly, while being immunized against feline enteritis, Taga was given an overdose of the relevant drug and died. At once I began to look for another female cub.

There are many exaggerated stories about the ferocity and treachery of leopards, and I hoped that by sharing the life of a leopardess young enough to become imprinted on me and by noting the behavior of her litters, I might be able to clear the species of its bad reputation. I also wanted to repeat with leopards the experiments I had made with lions and cheetahs, thus completing my study of the three great African cats.

The ancient Sumerians kept leopards as pets, and over the ages they have not been the only ones to do so. As a result a great deal is known about the behavior of leopards in captivity though comparatively little is known of their habits in the wild—and that little has caused them to be regarded as very dangerous animals.

In his book about leopards, Peter Turnbull Kemp collated most of the known facts about them, while Patrick Hamilton made a two-year study of leopards in Tsavo West National Park and was able to note new facts about their movements and behavior. His observations were made from a car or an airplane and he was aided by the use of telemetric radio collars attached to the animals he was studying. To his invaluable book I hoped to add complementary research not only on biological matters but on such subjects as how leopards control their breeding and whether they communicate by telepathy. These were subjects I had studied in lions and cheetahs. I hoped that in the end my work would result in some discovery that might be useful to humanity.

I knew it was going to be a hard task to find a female cub who combined all the qualities I required for my study. I was therefore thrilled when, on September 12, 1972, I received a telegram from Father Botta, a Catholic priest and an old friend, telling me that he had a 4-week-old female leopard cub who needed a home. It was he who, seven years earlier, had given me little Taga, and he knew how desperately I wanted another cub.

Father Botta was then stationed at a remote Mission in semidesert country, about 350 kilometers from my home at Naivasha. As soon as I received his telegram I set off for the Mission. When I saw the cub I fell in love with her and I named her Taga II. At the sight of me she vanished under a wardrobe that stood on the cement floor of the room in which she was kept during the day.

Later Father Botta told me how he had rescued the cub from some Africans who had killed the mother to sell her pelt. They had taken her two tiny cubs and given them to Father Botta in exchange for a goat. One of them died from dog bite wounds almost immediately, but he succeeded in rearing the other in spite of the fact that for several days she would not eat. Thereafter, with a lot of coaxing she consented to take zebra meat and cow's milk but required a daily laxative to stimulate her digestion.

During the day, she was locked in the cold, austere room I had seen her in; here she was fed in turn by whichever Sister happened to be free. After sunset she was led into a small walled garden where she spent the nights alone.

Hoping to make friends with her I asked if she could sleep with me. As it turned out it proved to be a very busy night for both of us, because Taga needed constant attention. Leopards have the fastest reactions of all cats!

Next morning we set off very early for Elsamere. The cub spent part of the journey on my knee and part on the grass bed I had made for her in the back of the car. As I drove I considered the best way of providing her with a comfortable home, spacious enough for her to exercise herself in until the time came when, as I hoped, I would take her into the bush for her return to the wild. Obviously I would need to build a large enclosure, wired in across the top to prevent her from climbing out.

When we arrived in the small township of Naivasha I contacted all the local contractors to find out if any of them could come out to Elsamere to build the boma. None could do so at such short notice, nor could any of those in Nairobi whom I contacted by telephone. Wondering how I was going to solve my problem I went to a grocer's shop where I bought a baby's bottle, some bone meal, and some cod-liver oil; then, as I had had no food since I left the Mission, I treated myself to an ice-cream cone. To eat it I retired into a corner. Suddenly I felt a touch on my shoulder and heard a woman's voice inquiring whether it wasn't uncomfortable eating my ice cream in a shop? Turning, I recognized Mrs. Morson, the wife of an old friend of George's whom I had met only once. In my dusty safari coat and with my mouth full of ice cream, I told her about my problem and took her to the car to see the cub. At once she suggested that I should follow her home where we would find her husband; she would ask him if their carpenter could help in building the enclosure.

Though I knew the Morsons so slightly, they came instantly to my aid and this incident proved to be the beginning of a long friendship. Equipped with a tape measure, we drove straight to Elsamere and chose a site. It was on the lawn near my bedroom so that, should the little leopard need help during the night, I would hear any cry she gave. I had, however, to face the fact that even if the Morsons' carpenter and a team of workmen from one of our neighbors started on the job at once, it would take three weeks before the enclosure could be completed. Meanwhile, by night the cub lay around my neck like a scarf. This she loved doing, as had the first Taga. Of course, it is a fact that all young animals, including babies, need tactile contact with their mother; if they are deprived of it, they often turn into neurotic adults. Until now the little leopard had not had a real foster-mother because at the Mission she had been looked after by too many different Sisters. I was happy that she accepted me quickly and became attached to me.

While the noisy process of building went on it was impossible for us to play on the lawn by day, so I kept Taga secured behind the glass doors of the large verandah through which she could watch the birds and the Colobus monkeys in the trees, while herself basking in the sun. In the early mornings and the late afternoons, before the workmen had come and after they had left, I took the cub around the garden to give her exercise. Inquisitively she inspected every bush looking for a suitable hideout and jumped onto the obsidian rocks which looked like black glass jutting out of the lawn. Eventually she chose one close to the lake from which she could watch the waterfowl and catch the last glow of the setting sun. She was also intrigued by a pile of wooden posts that were to be used for building her boma; after heaving herself to the top of the stack she enjoyed slithering to the bottom or hiding between the posts.

Naturally Elsamere's small forest with its dense undergrowth attracted her, and I had to keep a very strict lookout to insure that she did not make a dash for it. I tried to put a collar around her neck with a leash attached to it but stopped quickly when, outraged, she defended her freedom with such piercing screams it was difficult to believe that they could be made by so small an animal. The more she moved around with me the less she liked being restrained. Very soon she developed a strong personality (or should it be animality?) and I found myself once again confronted with the delicate task of winning a young animal's cooperation rather than enforcing her obedience; yet, at the same time, I had to show clearly who was boss.

For the second week I kept Taga inside a crate which had formerly belonged to Pippa. She was naturally clean, so rather than mess up her box she always gave a low miaow when she wanted to be taken out. On one such occasion I carried her onto the lawn; it was then dark, and when I put her down she ran off and scrambled up an acacia tree from which I would have had no chance of dislodging her unless I grabbed her at once. When I tried to pull her down she struggled and fell about 2 meters to the lawn. As she started to limp away, I picked her up and put her back into her crate. I was worried next morning when I saw that she was still limping, so I called the vet who lived near Nairobi. He arrived within two hours and diagnosed a fracture but wished to take an X-ray to discover just how bad the break was. He was surprised that so short a fall should have resulted in a broken leg and said that her bones must be abnormally brittle. This he attributed to a shortage of calcium, probably due to being fed on zebra meat, which lacked the hemoglobin and phosphorus of a natural kill, and also perhaps to having lived on a cold cement floor while at the Mission. From now on, I was told, Taga should have a diet different from the one I had been giving her, which consisted of freshly killed mole-rats, Farex, bone meal, diluted Nestlé's milk, and Abidec vitamins. Other supplementary vitamins would now be needed as well as plenty of milk. Also, until her boma was completed she should be out of doors as much as possible. But first I had to take her to the laboratory at Kabete for the X-ray.

The vet advised me to put her into a plastic bag, leaving the zipper partly open to admit fresh air. I did this and then placed her on the passenger seat of my car. I patted her now and then to assure her that I was nearby and she settled down contentedly. The X-ray showed only a minor break, which should knit within two or three weeks if she was treated with the medicines the vet prescribed. To buy them I had to drive into Nairobi. There it took me some time to find a shady place to park the car. With Taga settled in the bag, I left the window two inches open and then went off to shop, but suddenly I became worried that the cub, realizing she had been deserted, would struggle and attract the attention of a passerby, who might try to force the open window. I therefore went back and closed the window. When I returned after an hour and a half, no sound came from the bag and there was no movement in it. Frantically I tore at the zipper, which was jammed by torn lining. Taga was dead.

In this tragic way I learned that the oxygen in a closed, parked car is soon exhausted and that as a result people have lost their pets and even their babies. Judging by the wet, torn shreds of lining, Taga must have struggled to get more air, become entangled, and died of suffocation. We had shared only twelve days, but they had been days of great happiness. I buried her next to her favorite obsidian rock. Even though the vet assured me that she would never have grown into the strong, healthy leopard I needed for my research, I suffered great remorse.

On my return from a visit to London I found that Taga's boma had been completed and this constantly reminded me of the tragedy. But I still lived in hope of acquiring another female leopard cub. Until that happened the boma could serve as a nursery for various wild animals in need of help. For eight months it was occupied by a jackal with a badly broken leg which had been sent to me by George, and it was followed by one of the Verreaux's eagle owls which had broken a wing in a fight with a fish eagle. Then came two baby Colobus monkeys in need of protection from the fish eagles; they remained in the boma for six months before I was able to release them.

During the years 1970 to 1977 I had to put aside my leopard project, for I was the victim of a series of accidents: I had five major operations on my right hand, which had been crushed in a car accident, and in the end I had to resign myself to losing its use. Then I broke my right elbow and subsequently my right knee and later my right ankle, besides having to have an operation for a hip replacement. Because I had to be within reach of medical treatment I needed to live mainly at our home on Lake Naivasha.

Of course I had plenty to keep me busy: helping to promote the Elsa Appeals in various countries, writing *Pippa's Challenge* and *Joy Adamson's Africa*, helping with the filming of *Living Free, Forever Free,* and the TV serial of *Born Free.* I was also able to accept invitations to Hungary and the U.S.S.R. to learn how wildlife conservation was conducted in those countries. In spite of these many occupations I never lost my ambition to undertake a leopard project and I regarded these years simply as an interlude which I must accept until the day came when I could again camp out in the bush. Meanwhile, when I could, I put my time to good use searching for a suitable spot to conduct my experiment when I should be fit again and when I had secured a suitable leopard cub.

In 1975 I bought a Toyota Land-Cruiser and drove it on its maiden trip some 435 kilometers to Shaba, which is close to Samburu Game Reserve. I thought this might be a suitable location for releasing a leopard and it would indeed have been perfect for the purpose had it not been for the presence of the Shifta, gangs of guerrillas-cum-poachers who were based in the Shaba Mountains from which they descended to loot and murder. The Isiolo Councilors insisted that even for our reconnaissance we should be accompanied by an escort of four armed Rangers; later, when I saw footprints of the Shifta all over the ground, I realized that this had been a wise precaution.

It was sad that the security risk made the area unsuitable for my project, for in all other respects it was ideal: rocky hills, forested plains, several springs, a river by which to camp, enough prey for a leopard to feed on, a few potential mates living in the mountains, and finally, for my convenience, Isiolo with its shops and post office only 50 kilometers away.

My next recce took me to Tsavo West National Park. The Director was in favor of my project and kindly lent me a plane to help me find a suitable campsite, if not in Tsavo West then in Tsavo East. The authorities had no objection to my camping in one or other of the Parks but when I told them that my rehabilitation project might last for two or three years they asked me to promise that I would never under any circumstances ask for any assistance from them. It has always been a principle of mine not to become dependent on anyone—let alone become a nuisance to the local officials—but in such a long-term study how could I be certain that an emergency might not arise and that I might not need help? I had to abandon the idea of choosing one of the Tsavo Parks.

In 1976 I made two trips to Mara Game Reserve, 230 kilometers from Elsamere, on the recommendation of the Director. The local authorities were most helpful but all the places where I might have camped near a spring were used by the Masai for watering their stock. Also, tourists were allowed to drive anywhere they pleased, so Mara Reserve proved really unsuitable for my project. I felt depressed, but certainly not defeated.

CHAPTER ONE

Penny Arrives

Up to now I had been searching for a venue for my study but I still had no leopard to rehabilitate. It was on November 11, 1976, that, most unexpectedly, I heard of a cub.

Since "the Elsa days" Sir Julian and Lady Huxley had been friends. She was now in Kenya to celebrate the thirtieth anniversary of UNESCO, which her husband had founded, and I decided to take her and two friends on a short safari to Lake Nakuru to see the flamingos. While observing a spoonbill we were driving across the treacherous white salt crust which edges the water when, with a squelch, the car stopped and sank up to its hub caps in the mud.

We stuffed rags and even some of our clothing under the spinning wheels but this did no good; so next we collected dry grass and brushwood, yet in spite of all our efforts the car sank still lower. When it began to get dark there was nothing left to do but to try to find the nearest Ranger's Post. I had a vague recollection that some time ago I had seen a house standing among trees about 7 or 8 kilometers from the place where we were stuck and that this was the Post. As Juliette Huxley was nearly eighty years old and my leg was still in plaster, our friends gallantly offered to set out in the dark to get help. We stayed in the car, switching the lights off and on to guide them. To our great relief, they returned after three hours accompanied by two Rangers and a Land-Rover, which pulled our car onto firm ground. We all had a drink to celebrate the rescue and it was while this was going on that I learned from the Rangers that there was a tiny leopard cub at the Park's H.Q.

Fortunately I knew the Divisional Game Warden of the area from the time when I was rehabilitating Pippa in Meru Park and he was Assistant Warden there. We were good friends, so I hoped he would help me to get the cub. Next day I returned and made some inquiries; I learned that the little leopard was a female who had been found by a hunting party, after apparently being abandoned by its mother or, more likely, orphaned. The men had handed it in to the nearest Ranger and he had brought it to the Nakuru Park Ranger's H.Q. This had happened about a month before; the cub was now thought to be around two months old. She was beautiful, and judging by her size and dark coloring I thought she must be a forest leopard and was more likely to be 3 than 2 months old. The cub had been named Jenny and was being looked after by a young Ranger, named Charles, who fed her three times a day on raw liver and milk into which a teaspoonful of calcium lactate, the same amount of bone meal, and a drop of Bendex had been added. She had already been vaccinated twice against feline enteritis and was due for a third injection in January. Jenny lived in an outdoor enclosure next to the Warden's house and was taken for walks in the mornings and the afternoons. As a result of all this attention, she was in excellent condition.

As she looked inquisitively at me, I could hardly believe my luck. Here was my chance to get exactly what I had wanted for so long: a female cub, young enough for me to be imprinted on her, and already used to solid food. The Warden, knowing that I had waited for seven years to get just such a cub, very kindly arranged for me to have Jenny on loan from the government so that I would be able to study leopard behavior in the same way that I had studied lion and cheetah behavior. He also offered to let Charles come to Elsamere for a little time to allow Jenny, while still accompanied by someone familiar, to get used to her new home and foster-mother.

On November 26 she arrived with "nanny" Charles and her own blanket and feeding bowl. I changed her name to Penny, which sounded very like Jenny but was easier to project over a long distance. In doing this I was taking into account the possibility of one day having to search for her in the bush.

The boma at Elsamere was much bigger than the enclosure she had been used to and the cub instantly inspected every part of it; she was far too excited to look at the food we offered her, much less eat it. We waited till it got dark, then brought more food, and this she ate, though only a very little. At nine o'clock we thought that she must have settled down and went out to visit her. We found her very much awake; indeed, she gave me a good nip in the leg.

Knowing that a predator should eat a complete kill with the blood and viscera still warm, the next morning I gave her a freshly killed rabbit. She played with the carcass but did not know how to open it, so we did it for her. Immediately she tore out the intestines and ate all the viscera before starting on the solid flesh and the bones. While doing this she accidentally bit and scratched me with her razor-sharp teeth and claws. Luckily, as I have an exceptionally thin skin and only need to bang myself against a hard object to start bleeding, I always carry sulphanilamide powder in my pocket, so I was able to disinfect the wounds and stop the bleeding immediately.

With Penny's arrival the four Colobus monkeys who lived at Elsamere, and are so tame they take carrots and tidbits from my hand, disappeared for a few days, as did the eagle owls who used to come in the evening to eat chicken heads which I got for them from a nearby farm. Indeed, I now had a sense of a hush surrounding Elsamere. It seemed that among the wildlife the word had got about: "There is a leopard around and a leopard is a leopard and should be avoided."

Penny loved her new home and spent most of her time on one of the wooden platforms I had rigged up for her in each corner of the boma as a substitute for the trees on which in natural conditions she would rest. She loved going for walks on the 3-acre lawn that surrounds the house. Only a few trees grow there; the rest of Elsamere consists of a wooded plain and a natural forest that has become the refuge of bushbuck, reedbuck, duiker, dik-dik (antelope), marsh mongoose, genet, and white-tailed mongoose, all of which have found food, shelter, and safety from snares and hunting dogs there.

The forest was a great temptation to Penny. She would have loved to hide in its thick undergrowth, but if she had done so we should never have found her. I had therefore to train her to walk on a lead. I expected her to struggle, as puppies do before accepting such control, but to my amazement she quickly accepted the harness and the lead and moreover never got entangled in it.

Most of the day she spent under a shady tree on the lawn, sleeping close to Charles or playing. To vary her diet the gardener caught mole-rats for her which she loved and ate whole, rejecting only their sharp teeth. With the onset of the rains, fierce safari ants made their appearance. Charles poured engine oil over them, which suffocates them instantly, but he had not counted on Penny's reaction. Though she always carefully avoided live ants she delighted in rolling in the sticky mess and it took us many days to rid her pelt of the oil even though she cooperated by turning herself around so that we could rub each side of her coat with grass and rags.

I was interested to observe that, when feeding, Penny used a position similar to that of a cheetah: both crouch low with their elbows tucked in whereas a lion holds his food with his forepaws.

After Penny had been at Elsamere a week she threw a fit which lasted for five minutes, white foam dribbling from her mouth. Alarmed, I called Dr. Paul Sayer at the Kabete Laboratories in Nairobi. For many years he has been our friend as well as our vet. He thought she was probably suffering from hookworm and told us to give her one and a half tablets of Cannex in the morning and the same dose in the afternoon. Penny seemed to know that we were trying to help her and never bit or scratched us when we were dosing her; indeed, she was unusually gentle. That she was off-color and lethargic during the following days we attributed to the treatment; but six days later she threw another fit and her tummy was tight as a drum. Paul Sayer told us to stop feeding her liver and pulped rabbit bones and give her the maximum dose of calcium. He now thought it possible that a sharp bone might have lacerated her stomach.

In spite of this change of diet Penny's coat became duller and duller, and although I gave her liquid paraffin daily she was constipated. During all this time she was touchingly affectionate and even after dark when she would normally have been too boisterous for me to play with her she responded to my caresses with a gentle pawing and allowed me to use her shoulder as a pillow when I rested close to her. A week later she had a third fit and by then her condition had plainly deteriorated. An examination of her blood showed that she had an infection of hemobartonella, a very vicious parasite. To treat her we needed to administer four one-gram capsules of tetracycline every twenty-four hours for fourteen days.

During this anxious time Penny's only amusement was watching the Colobus monkeys. Having seen me playing with her, they must have realized that "the terror of Africa" would be harmless so long as they were separated by wire. Gradually they came nearer to the boma, hop-

ping onto its posts and finally onto the roof. Penny made frantic efforts
to reach them and excelled in acrobatics, particularly in mid-air twists.
The monkeys learned exactly how to time their teasing leaps; even so,
they were lucky not to lose some hair from their long tails. Soon the
game became a daily ritual which both sides enjoyed. I was glad that
it provided Penny with a break in her monotonous routine while confined within the boma. When she was able to go for walks we had to be
very careful to see if the monkeys were around, for she was extremely
keen on getting at them and had become very strong. Indeed, by now
I found it difficult to control her with my one functioning hand; also,
my broken ankle was mending very slowly.

Under the circumstances, I asked if Charles could stay on at Elsamere
until I could find an assistant. Penny liked him and he was good with
her; my only criticism was that when he wanted her to move he jumped
and danced in front of her with such gusto that she, in imitation,
jumped at him and at me so vigorously that we needed always to be on
the alert and could never afford to be off guard in case she landed on us.

After four days of the new treatment Penny's blood smears showed
that she was free of the parasite. From then on we fed her in the
mornings on as much raw meat as she would eat; into it we mixed bone
meal, calcium phosphate, Farex, and a little salt. In the evenings we
gave her two chickens which had died of respiratory trouble at a nearby
farm but were otherwise perfectly healthy. With each meal we gave her
milk into which four drops of Abidec were added twice weekly. Three
times a week she had a freshly killed and skinned rabbit. Like a wild
leopard she carried the carcass, not to a tree since there were none in
her boma, but to one of the platforms. Obviously she did this to protect
her kill from predators. It was interesting that this instinct to store food
had developed in her before she had learned to kill. Lions and cheetahs
begin to teach their cubs to kill only when they have grown their
permanent teeth. In the case of lions this occurs when they are 17
months old (after that it of course takes some months before they become efficient killers). Cheetahs start to teach their offspring to kill at
14 months but the cubs remain dependent on their mother till they are
$17\frac{1}{2}$ months old.

From little Taga I had learned that a leopard's deciduous teeth are
fully developed at 6 weeks and now from Penny I learned that their
permanent teeth make their appearance when they are 5 months old.
At this age her instinct for killing had still not developed, but from the
first she knew how to protect her food. She demonstrated this by

straddling her blanket with her front legs when she wanted to move it, and covering it with her body in the way that later she would use to move a kill.

Knowing that all cats need roughage, in the form of skin and feathers, I tried to feed Penny rabbit skins and chicken feathers, but she would not touch either. Indeed, she carefully plucked the chickens, with the result that the ground inside the boma looked like a snowfield. When there was a wind she greatly enjoyed chasing the feathers around.

She also had fun running after tennis balls brought her by a five-year-old boy who often came to play with her. I am sure that all animals are aware of our feelings toward them and respond accordingly. Thus a child who has not been told that certain animals are dangerous and who, consequently, is not afraid of them, and regards all animals as friends, will find that the animals respond in a friendly way. In this case the boy's parents did not wish him to enter the boma, so he and Penny ran up and down with the wire between them till both were out of breath.

Like all young animals, Penny fretted when she was alone. Her most active times were early in the morning and after sunset. We took her for a walk between 7:00 and 9:00 A.M., by which time it had become very hot and she did not want to move. To coax her back to her boma and her morning meal we had to wriggle a rabbit skin tied to a string in front of her. Once home and fed she dozed off close to Charles. At tea time we again took her for a walk, but on this second expedition she never showed as much energy as in the morning, and often only wished to climb a tree or to play with the water sprinkler on the lawn.

Penny was a very good tree climber, and we encouraged this sport by hiding the rabbit skin in some branches. She was very proud when she found and retrieved it, and used to parade it in front of us until we patted her. Then she would drop it and seem to ask for the game to be repeated. The cub was very affectionate and never scratched me except by accident, usually when she was nibbling me playfully, as she would have nibbled at her mother's thick skin. If I checked her with a firm "No" she would instantly put her two paws into her mouth and nibble at them as though to say: "Nibble I must, but I'll bite my own paws rather than make you cross." This sight always disarmed me. Penny often embraced me with her claws well tucked in, but unfortunately I could never rely on their being retracted; Charles, who had a thicker skin, never got scratched. Penny certainly never intended to draw blood.

For stretching her tendons and sharpening her claws she had a daily ritual: she stood on her hind legs, close to a certain tree which had rough bark, and stretched herself as high as she could along the trunk, then drew her paws slowly downwards; afterwards the marks of her claws could be seen on the bark. Gradually our walks became longer; no more did we keep to the neighborhood of the house, but went into the bush-covered plain.

Luckily Elsamere had 50 acres that were of no agricultural use; they consisted of an obsidian lava flow which had emanated from a distant volcano. Because it could only support grazing for three cows, this area had been for sale when we bought the property. Since what we wanted was a home and privacy and we had no intention of running a farm, we had bought the land. It proved to be an ideal playground for Penny; here she could get plenty of exercise, climb trees, ambush us from behind bushes, observe birds and small antelope, and all this at an altitude and in a climate similar to that of her birthplace.

As an interim playground it was perfect, but she needed a permanent home, and I knew I must hurry to look for one.

CHAPTER TWO

The Search
for a Home

THE LONG-AWAITED merger of Kenya's National Parks and her Game Department had taken place the previous November, but before the new Wildlife and Conservation Management Department was announced, many changes in staff took place, and, inevitably, decisions on projects like my leopard study were delayed.

I thought, however, that I should do all I could to investigate the possibilities of a home for Penny and decided to try my luck with Amboseli. I flew there simply for the purpose of discussing the project with the Warden before making an application to the authorities. I could not have received a warmer welcome, but as I drove around I did not need his warning that Penny would not survive there even for a week. I saw the tracks of tourists' cars everywhere, and, as well, posses of Masai trekking with their livestock; under the circumstances, I was not surprised to hear macabre stories of poaching.

Undeterred by having written off Amboseli as a possible area for Penny's rehabilitation, I now ordered a radio collar in case we had to rehabilitate her in a place where tracking was difficult. Meanwhile I had been in correspondence for some time with a twenty-year-old American student who thought that being involved in such a unique project might help him in his career as a zoologist and so offered to join me as an assistant. David arrived from the United States at the beginning of February 1977. From the start he had a good rapport with Penny and after a few days was able to take over from Charles, who then returned to Nakuru.

While all this was happening, Penny had not only the Colobus monkeys to amuse her but also three cheeky young white-tailed mongooses who used to sneak into the boma when she was out to steal any scraps of meat that were lying around. Aware of what was happening in her absence, she became even more alert to every movement in the forest undergrowth.

By now she was losing her fluffy baby coat, and seemed to like me to stroke the loose hairs off her. Her pelt had developed a glossy, bluish sheen; with her square rosettes, which started at the root of the tail and followed her spine up to the shoulders, she was extremely handsome. As I saw her playing with the elegant black-and-white Colobus monkeys while being watched from high up in the trees by the Verreaux's eagle owls—the largest and handsomest owls of Africa—I thought how lucky I was to have these beautiful creatures living at Elsamere and accepting me as their friend.

Of course Penny was still living the life of a pet, but I was glad to see that her instincts were not impaired. For instance, however heavy the rain, she would always stand out in the open on one of her platforms; she never sought refuge in her hut.

Since Charles had left she rarely jumped at us, and seemed happiest on our walks or when we sat close to her, stroking her or de-ticking her. Certainly she knew that she was loved and cared for. Gradually we took her for longer walks to places where she could sniff at dik-dik droppings. When she did this she pulled up her top lip in order to expose her olfactory glands and make the most of the scent.

By mid-February I was still without any news from the authorities about where I could rehabilitate Penny, so I accepted the offer of a neighboring farmer to bring her to his land, which was ideal leopard country. He kindly offered to drive us to the place. On our way we passed through hills and plains, thick bush, and a forest with open glades; then we came to an escarpment with impressive cliffs and here we walked along thickly forested ravines with delightful rivulets. This was ideal for wild leopards, of which there were plenty, but it was obvious that, even with a radio collar, Penny would be impossible to trace in this type of territory. Besides, there were the nearby farms to consider, not to mention the ever-present poachers. Under the circumstances I felt obliged to re-fuse the tempting offer.

Soon afterwards I received a letter from the authorities saying that they considered my leopard project important and had designated Tsavo East as a site. I went there a second time, but a terrible drought had devastated the area and I saw no future for Penny in Tsavo.

As the weeks passed, various possibilities were suggested and I visited a number of areas, but nothing came of these schemes. It was now April 15, and Penny was growing fast. Like a lion, she had a 3-millimeter hairy tip to her tail. I observed that she had a slight squint, but when I studied photographs of other leopards I realized that this was a charac-teristic of the species. I wondered whether it might be useful in confusing a prey that was being hunted. Personally, I found it very attractive; Penny's eyes were smaller and more slanted than those of a lion or cheetah, and often when she almost closed them they became slits that, in the camouflage of her mask, were practically invisible.

By now we had started taking her for walks in the hilly hinterland. To reach it we had to cross the road that went to the lake and which cut through the grounds of Elsamere. Penny was nervous of the road, but once we had coaxed her to cross it she became very playful in the wooded hills. Here she could ambush us, investigate rocky outcrops, sniff at mole-rat mounds, and roll in strongly scented plants. We assumed that the rolling was for the purpose of disguising her own scent. Elsa and Pippa used to roll in the droppings of their prey for the same reason. At times Penny would stop and gaze across the lake at the vast expanse of the Rift Valley while rubbing herself affectionately against our legs.

Unfortunately our walks came to an end when the waterhole at Elsa-mere had to be repaired. This involved a team of workmen erecting a heavy rig at the site, and the resulting noise of drilling, not to mention that of shouted orders, panicked Penny. She refused to leave her boma until the work was completed and the team had gone. Even then, several weeks passed before she would venture onto the plain; indeed, so great was her apprehension that when we reached the road she defecated and bolted. After she was recaptured, David would have to carry her over the crossing.

She much preferred the hills to the plain, and took longer walks in that region, but regularly at 10:00 A.M. she sat down and refused to budge. Up to now we had given her her morning meal before her walk, and as a result when she got hot there was no reason for her to move until the temperature fell. Therefore we often found ourselves stranded wherever she had flopped down. As this could be tiresome, we changed our routine and took her on pre-breakfast walks, so that when she became hungry we could coax her back to the boma.

I was interested to see that during the day she never dropped her feces in the boma but always outside, in certain specific places. Of course during the night she was obliged to foul her home, but we cleaned it up in the morning.

At this stage of her development, though this was to change, Penny was never in the least upset when we wore clothes that were unfamiliar to her. Elsa and Pippa, on the other hand, invariably had bolted when we appeared in garments they had not seen before.

On the whole the little leopard was cooperative as well as affectionate, but when she did not get her way she would try to outwit us by washing herself endlessly, so that we got bored waiting for her, ceased to concentrate our attention on her, and then found that often she had done what she had intended to do. At this game she was always the winner. Penny was much more independent than either Elsa's or Pippa's cubs had been at her age and it was a challenge to try to understand the causes of her occasionally unpredictable behavior.

As human beings, we are inclined to judge animal intelligence by our own standards, not taking into account the fact that we know little about how their senses differ from our own. Unknown to us, every species has different needs for its survival, and these are usually beyond our perception. All we can do is try to learn from their behavior what triggers their reactions. In this context we should remember that some creatures have survived for four hundred million years, adapting themselves to a changing environment, and this should make us humble since we humans appeared only about three million years ago.

As for Penny, even though she was often enigmatic, we shared certain of her habits, one instance being that we both mark our territory—though certainly not in the same manner! At 5½ months she jetted for the first time. Her tail outstretched (like a lion or a cheetah), she propelled a milky liquid from her anal glands and marked a bush that stands some two hundred meters from my signpost at the entrance to the drive into Elsamere.

Before Penny's arrival I had often seen leopard spoors, not only on the hills but also crossing the road into the property. Now I thought that a wild leopard must have left his scent on the bush, and Penny wished to establish the fact that it was her territory. Later she sprayed more bushes along the boundary of Elsamere, and did this every time we passed by them. I noticed that the instinct to defend her territory seemed to develop at the moment when her permanent teeth appeared.

I had kept Elsa's deciduous canines, and now found it interesting to compare them with a leopard's milk canines. The leopard's were almost twice as long. Elsa had cooperated when I tried to help her get rid of her last baby teeth; now Penny did the same by opening her mouth as I wriggled a tooth loose. She did so again when her other canines were ready to go. I kept some of these.

While changing her teeth she was often off-color, reluctant to play, let alone walk, and had much difficulty in chewing her food, so much so that I tried to hand-feed her. At this time her temperature, instead of being between 101° and 102°, was 103°. It took great patience to hand-feed her and insure that she had enough food to avoid a loss of condition. After this experience, I can well believe that teething troubles are often responsible for a high mortality among leopard cubs.

Hoping to restrict her contact with strangers to a minimum during the period before her rehabilitation to the bush, I asked my visitors to keep away from her boma and to watch her only from a distance.

Penny showed a marked dislike for dark-skinned people. She was much less alarmed by people with white skin. This puzzled me because her first "nanny," Charles, whom she loved, was an African. I had observed the same reaction in other wild animals, and can only imagine that it may be an inherited trait arising from the fact that they had been hunted and trapped, often by cruel means, for centuries by Africans. Later, of course, the whites arrived and hunted them with guns, but often in circumstances in which they had no knowledge of where the bullet had come from.

So long as she was safely in her boma, Penny did not mind my African staff doing their daily chores near her, but once free, she bolted from them. Since groups of Africans talking in loud voices often walked along the public road on which, of course, there were also rattling trucks, this was enough to explain her fear.

I had become very depressed about finding a permanent home for Penny when one day a message came to me from the Warden of Samburu Game Reserve, telling me that he was interested in the project. The Reserve belonged to the Samburu Council and I would, of course, need their consent before introducing Penny into their area. Convinced that any condition they might impose would be preferable to settling in Tsavo, I set off on May 26 for the 340-kilometer drive.

Passing through Isiolo, I learned that Makedde, our former game scout who had worked under George for many years and had helped us with Elsa, had retired and was now looking for a job. I would need a Ranger to accompany us in the bush who was a good shot and could frighten away wild animals that might otherwise charge us. In fact, we had only had to do this twice in the ten years I had shared with Elsa and Pippa, but it was nevertheless a necessary precaution. On one occasion we met a rhino and her calf advancing toward us, and on another we came upon a sleeping buffalo concealed behind a bush which, if startled, might well have charged. Makedde shot over their heads and sent them running away. He was not only an experienced Ranger and a good tracker, but a man who never lost his head. He was also very knowledgeable about wild animals and very fond of them. I offered the old Turkana the job and he accepted instantly, promising to return with me to Naivasha on the following day.

This was a good beginning, and my meeting with the Warden was also very encouraging. He suggested a good campsite for us and agreed to build the camp, provided that the authorities gave their consent to the plan.

While driving with the Warden through the Park, I noticed that he had only one vehicle in which to travel around the Isiolo and Samburu Reserves, both of which he administered. This had been given him two years ago by the Elsa Fund, and it was now nearly worn out. I told him to send in an application for a new Land-Rover and that I would recommend that the Trustees of the Elsa Appeal purchase it for him.

When we returned to Elsamere I introduced Makedde to Penny. For an hour she watched him while he stood outside the boma. Then she allowed him to enter, and even to stroke her. Since it was the middle of the day, she was sleepy. Later, during our walk, she tripped him playfully, and during her evening meal let him come close to her.

Next morning, to our surprise, she bolted at the sight of him, was extremely nervous, and there was no chance of his being allowed to touch her. For some days her reactions varied. Finally she accepted him and followed him on our walks so long as he strode ahead and she was able to watch him; if he walked behind her she bolted. She would only allow him to feed her if she was at home on her platform. Makedde treated her with great patience but she never allowed him the familiarities she accepted from David and myself.

Her way of showing her affection for me was by holding my leg between her strong front paws or nibbling at my ankles and sometimes sitting on my foot to prevent me from moving. I let her take the initiative about where she wished to walk, hoping that these walks would become the highlight of her otherwise boring life in the boma.

When sunset came her pupils dilated and she became very excited and restless. We then left her alone. Had we remained with her she would have jumped at us and we would have been obliged to punish her. Our happy relationship would have been spoiled. It was sad that we had to abandon her after dark, which was when she most needed our company, but there was no alternative.

Unfortunately my elation at the prospect of releasing Penny in Samburu Park was short-lived, because it was not long before I was told that the authorities considered the area too small. The only alternative seemed to be Tsavo, which seemed hopeless to me. This also upset David, who told me he had lost interest in Penny and would leave at once. I was in a very awkward situation. Penny had become too strong for me to control. If we surprised a dik-dik, or, worse still, a reedbuck, she would pull with such violence that her chain would rip the skin off my fingers and I would be obliged to let her go. In such a situation all I could hope was that she would not chase the antelope onto my neighbor's land. On several occasions I managed to hold onto the chain but then Penny broke the harness.

Another complication was that during the recent rain the grass had grown hip-high, concealing many ant-bear holes as well as the runners of the star grass, which are as strong as steel. During our expeditions alone I often tripped over these or was pulled over by Penny. She plainly thought that this was part of a game and so added to the fun by jumping on me. As we wrestled in the high, wet grass I could only hope and pray that my implanted steel hip would not be damaged. To protect myself from Penny's sharp claws I added to my canvas elbow-length gloves a canvas apron. In this outfit, plus gumboots, I must have looked ridiculous, but at least I escaped scratches.

Fortunately for me David now returned, and said he would stay till mid-August. This gave me some time in which to look for a new assistant. Meanwhile I visited the Director of Samburu Park, on whom the decision concerning Penny's future depended, and begged him to change his mind. I was not very hopeful but that evening I heard that I was to be allowed to take her to Shaba Reserve.

CHAPTER THREE

Building a Camp
in Shaba

SHABA RESERVE, COVERING an area of 100 square kilometers, had been cleared of local squatters and their livestock, for which a bore-hole had been drilled outside the boundary. It is adjacent to Isiolo and Samburu Game Reserves and is administered by the same Warden, whom I knew.

Now I had to meet him so that together we could decide on a campsite. Only after having done this could I write a formal application to the Isiolo Councilors asking them to approve my plan to conduct my leopard study in their new Reserve.

It was two years since I had visited Shaba. At that time it was being heavily poached and was often invaded by guerrillas; today it was peaceful and the Game Reserve was ready for tourists, though before they arrived there was need for more roads, campsites, and, one hoped, a lodge.

I knew Shaba well from the time George had been responsible for this area. I thought that if Penny could adapt to her new life there it would be an ideal location for her rehabilitation. It was only 60 kilometers from Meru, and it would enable me to study a leopard in conditions similar to those in which I had studied the lion and the cheetah. This was an important factor when making a comparison of the three great cats of Africa.

I got in touch with the Warden of Shaba, who seemed delighted to have Penny in his area. We selected an ideal campsite in a grove of acacia trees next to a spring which fed a swamp where buffalo, lion, oryx, zebra, Grant's gazelle, ostrich, and smaller birds came to drink.

A cart track led to the spring. To the north lay more swamps and plains intersected by ridges of lava. In the distance the Isiolo Mountains loomed like a line of ships. Beyond the acacia grove the land rose in a gentle slope covered with blocks of lava of all sizes and shapes between which grew thorny scrub and large acacia trees which would provide Penny with shade and cover. Up till now she had been living at Elsamere at an altitude of 1,938 meters, where the climate was cool and the vegetation lush. Would she endure a change of environment? Since I had exhausted all other possibilities and was well aware of the extraordinary adaptability of leopards—whose presence has been recorded in the highlands, in savannah, in rain forests, in the most arid regions of Africa, and also in the extreme climates of China, Manchuria, India, Russia, Anatolia, Mesopotamia, and Arabia—I decided to risk Shaba.

Now my concern was to hurry up the formalities so that Penny and I could reach her new home as soon as possible. I therefore wrote a formal application to the Isiolo Councilors and handed it in to the office clerk as I passed through on my return journey to Elsamere.

At the same time I recommended to the London Trustees of the Elsa Fund that they should release money to make an airstrip at Shaba. This would help the Warden to conduct aerial antipoaching control.

I had already asked an old friend to look out for a contractor who would be prepared to build the camp enclosure. Not long afterwards, James, someone we knew who was farming near Nanyuki, offered to do the job for us if we could supply him with a four-wheel pickup. We bought him a secondhand Toyota, which later on we used for collecting firewood and water. Since every day was precious I gave up the idea of having a house and settled for tents. A piece of luck was that many safari firms were selling their equipment because of the recent ban on hunting; thus I was able to buy the tents at a reasonable price, and also bought two refrigerators that worked on gasoline and various other camping necessities.

When recollecting those days I must mention help given me by Peter Johnson, a chartered accountant and the Chairman of the Elsa Advisory Committee of Kenya, who had been my financial adviser since the early days of the Elsa Fund. Now he gave me invaluable help with all the difficulties which arose in connection with Penny's rehabilitation. I appreciated this very much, the more so since I knew that Peter was personally against the project, believing, as did many of my friends, that it involved a great risk since leopards were known to be unpredictable and very dangerous. It was a legend that I hoped to kill.

While all this had been going on I was taking notes on Penny's behavior, and this taught me much about leopards; for instance, that the instinct for storing food develops before the instinct for hunting. I had also discovered the age at which a leopard starts to mark its territory, the age at which leopards change their teeth, that at which they lose their baby fluff, develop fur, and also their rosettes, and when they begin to be interested in chasing birds and small animals. I was fascinated to observe the importance they attach to disguising their scent. This they do by rolling in strongly scented plants such as Mexican marigold, *Leonotis*, *Nepeta folia*, or in an oily labiate creeper.

Recently Penny had discovered a large acacia tree. She loved this tree so much that she always pulled toward it whoever was leading her and then jumped as high as the lead would permit, straddling a branch and refusing to come down. From this position she had a splendid view down the plain. The only way of inducing her to move was by wriggling a rabbit skin attached to a string in front of her. This decoy resembled a live prey and she could not resist it; as a result it had become a necessity on our walks, for without it we could not induce her to move when she felt like staying put.

Penny was very conservative in her habits, stopping at certain places where there were bushes whose branches she chewed. Perhaps this helped her new teeth to come through. There were other places where she invariably rolled and washed herself. We used to refer to these places as Penny's *manyattas*, a word which in northern Kenya means a boma. She was always delighted if I made a fuss of her when she was in one of her *manyattas*. I stroked her sleek fur and spoke to her in a low voice, but was always on my guard, for at any moment she was liable to jump in the air and come at me with outstretched front paws. This would be followed by acrobatic turns until I let her go free. But even when she was bursting with energy, she seldom ran more than a few meters, then stopped and looked back, apparently waiting for me to pick up her leash. I was puzzled by her desire to free herself from the frustrating leash, and on the other hand by the sense of security she seemed to derive from knowing I was close by.

She loved retrieving the rabbit skin from a branch. We usually placed it in a position from which this was difficult. After carefully assessing the situation, she would perform extraordinary aerial acrobatics until she succeeded in shaking or breaking the branches and dislodging the pelt. Then she would look down at us as though saying, "See how clever I have been! Aren't you going to clap?"

Three candidates applied for the post of assistant to replace David. Since it was essential that Penny, as well as I, should interview them, I suggested that they join us on a walk; however, she tripped up the lot of them and showed no preference. I thought that a stranger would have had a very odd impression if he had watched the three candidates plus David and myself, all equipped with canvas gloves, following a young leopard across the plain. In the end I asked two of the men to come on trial and decided to make a final decision later in the hope that Penny would play her part.

If she had been born in mid-August 1976, she would now be one year old. Since leopards are supposed to develop more quickly than lions and cheetahs, I wondered if she might be near puberty; if she was, that might explain why she had now ceased to mark her territory. I even wondered whether she might be in oestrus.

Her wild instincts were certainly unimpaired. This became obvious when David found the body of a bat-eared fox that had just been run over by a car near our drive. The body was still warm and limp, and Penny became very excited. With head held high she straddled it and dragged it into her boma, where she hid it out of our view and guarded it all day. This was David's last present to Penny, since that evening he left for the United States.

I realized that she did not know how to open her kill, and decided to help her. I was amazed that she allowed me to pull the fox from under her and actually watched me skin it. This was a sign of tremendous trust. Eventually I held out her neatly prepared dinner for her. First she tore at the intestines, sucking them as though they were spaghetti, while pressing their contents out between her claws and teeth. Then she ate all the viscera and afterwards allowed me to hold the vertebrae of the carcass in the best position for her to chew the bones except those of the head and the bigger bones.

Until then, as I said, we had used a rabbit skin to lure her along on a walk, but from then on the skin of a bat-eared fox proved even more irresistible. She would, for instance, settle herself comfortably in the fork of one of her favorite trees while we threw the skin a little above her head. However difficult the position, she seldom failed to catch it. Recently we had seen her hook a bird through the wire netting of her boma and pull out a few feathers before the creature flew away. This made me realize how important catching a moving target would later become for Penny when she would largely depend on birds for her food. As she grew interested in hunting she showed us very clearly how much she disapproved of our talking during our walks with her, since this scared the game away.

It was now that I received a letter from the Isiolo Councilors asking me to attend a meeting on August 15 at which the plan for me to conduct my leopard project at Shaba would be discussed. Since I had not been able to start building the camp before I had received the Councilors' consent to the plan, and every day was precious, I asked if it might be possible to hold the meeting at an earlier date. The Councilors kindly changed it to August 4, and, still more generously, gave me permission to start building the camp at once.

Simultaneously a radio collar with all its telemetric accessories arrived from the United States. Little as I liked being dependent on a mechanical device, the nocturnal habits of leopards and the lava-strewn nature of the ground at Shaba, which might make spooring impossible, made me feel that a radio collar was a necessity.

The next few days were very busy ones. There were many meetings, I gave lectures to tourists, and had again to worry about finding a couple to occupy Elsamere, since the people who had offered to be caretakers earlier in the year had by now settled elsewhere. I also needed to find a cook. I was successful in both my searches. A very suitable couple contacted me and were prepared to live at Elsamere, and Kifosha, the cook who had been with us during the Elsa years, now offered to return. Not only was he an excellent cook, but he had a remarkably fine character.

On August 3 I drove in pouring rain the 300 kilometers to Nanyuki. There was no hotel at Isiolo, and I wanted to be sure of being at the meeting at 9:30 A.M. I had asked James, our farming friend, to drive me to Isiolo and later to Shaba so that I could see how far he had got with the building of the camp.

During the 100-kilometer drive from Nanyuki to Isiolo we dropped from about 2,200 to 900 meters, and had a splendid view of the Samburu and Shaba Mountains.

It was twenty years since we had left Isiolo. That was after Elsa's death; she had come to us when George was the Warden in charge of the area. Our life in the bush had been fascinating, and it was further enriched by our interest in the young lioness. Fortunately I could not then guess that so soon after her death I would be catapulted into a world of publicity and that my life would no longer be my own. I was to become involved in lecture tours on all five continents, during which I met people in every walk of life and established relations with publishers and film producers. The most important outcome of this period was my founding of a global organization to protect wild animals—it bears Elsa's name. All these travels widened my horizons and stimulated my ideas, but often at the expense of my health. Sometimes I felt that I could only carry on by thinking of the peaceful and interesting life of the bush, of the many wonders that nature will reveal to us if we are responsive, and of the limitless space which offers a certain spiritual freedom. Having lived for twenty years very close to nature and then for the next twenty years in a world of man-made values, I now felt that, as has been written of Elsa, "she belonged to two worlds" is true also of me since I, too, belong to both, though there was no doubt in which world I have my roots.

Now, as I approached our former home at Isiolo, I was overwhelmed by nostalgia, from which I only escaped by reflecting that soon I would again be living the life I loved, if not with Elsa, at least with Penny. It was sad that I would not this time be sharing the experience with George, but he was too devoted to the ten lions with whom he shares his life at Kora to join me at Shaba, and, in any case, lions and leopards do not mix.

At the meeting at Isiolo were twenty Councilors, many of whom remembered George and spoke warmly of him. Present, too, were the District Commissioner and the Warden of Samburu, Isiolo, and Shaba Reserves. Some had traveled great distances to attend the meeting at which, of course, projects other than mine would also be discussed. The older Councilors wore flowing white robes in the Islamic tradition while the younger generation wore Western suits. After the opening formalities were over I was told that in appreciation of the Toyota and the donation for making the airstrip—both given by the Elsa Fund—all the fees normally paid by a team of research workers would in my case be remitted for a year. The speaker then went on with a twinkle in his eye to say that he hoped that more gifts, of which they had great need, would warrant further remissions. This statement was received with loud laughter.

After a while one of the older Councilors rose and asked for silence. Then, addressing me with great dignity, he said, "Please keep in daily touch with your leopard, as in spite of the recent hunting ban, leopard skins are still highly prized." I was expecting this warning and had prepared everything I could think of to protect Penny. I had ordered an expensive radio set which would enable us to connect instantly with the Warden if we or she were in trouble. I had helped to make the airstrip, and I had offered to contribute to an antipoaching camel unit. But in spite of all this I now realized that I could not give a one hundred percent guarantee that Penny would always be safe.

As soon as the meeting was over I followed James to the camp. He was driving the Toyota pickup and I was in the Peugeot 504. I was thus able to discover how it would cope with the rough ground. My caution proved wise when I had a flat tire and discovered that my jack was ineffective. Later the pickup, too, went on strike. Many hours passed before we were mobile again. It was dark by the time we entered Shaba. I found myself driving through dust that was knee-deep and nearly swallowed up the car. I could see only a few inches ahead, but I had to keep moving at all costs, for if I stopped the Peugeot would sink deeper into the dust and would be immobilized; so I churned ahead at full speed, paying no attention to a sinister smell of burning. It was now so dark that I was progressing along the hip-deep rut unable to see anything, and could only pray that I would not run into an elephant. Eventually I reached lava; this did not make for easy driving, but at least it was an improvement on the dust.

At long last I spotted a little flicker of light in the distance and knew that we were near the camp. When we reached it, James, who had gallantly followed me, swallowing the dust raised by the Peugeot, looked like a chimney sweep, as did I. Our parched throats could hardly respond to the warmth of welcome from the cook and the labor gang.

Later on, sipping tea and nibbling biscuits, we discussed our problems with them until midnight. How were our supplies to be transported over 160 kilometers? How were we going to get the cedar posts that were needed, and how would we manage to dig holes 2-feet deep to plant them in when making the fence around the camp? What would Shaba hold in store for us? It had taken seven years to get Penny, and then another year to find a suitable home for her. Now things seemed to be falling into place, but in my ears rang the wise old Councilor's warning: "Please keep in daily touch with your leopard, as in spite of the recent hunting ban, leopard skins are still highly prized."

Early in the morning I made an inspection of the surroundings of the camp. The entrance would be within 50 meters of the spring which James had lined with a 40-gallon drum to prevent the mud walls from falling in. Startled by the sight of this unexpected object, a lioness, coming to drink by night, had banged on the drum to the considerable alarm of those who heard it.

Within a few hundred yards of the spring was a thorny thicket, which, because of its nearness to the swamp and the shade it provided, was obviously used by many animals. Now I visualized Penny choosing it as her den during the heat of the day.

After breakfast James and I set off to try to find an approach road other than the dreadful track by which we had arrived. After plowing along for a short distance on dust tracks we came to a better surface, and after 15 kilometers, to one of the two gates which give access to the Shaba Reserve. I now suggested that James should return to the camp since I did not expect to meet any further difficulties. He, however, insisted on following me right up to Isiolo, another 45 kilometers.

The track was so winding that I slowed down to 30 kilometers an hour. Even so, I came to a sudden halt when the Peugeot nosed into a soft, deep, 3-foot-wide crack caused by the recent rains. That I was uninjured was due to the fact that my Peugeot was designed to diminish the impact of frontal collision. It was very fortunate that James was there to pull me out. He found the chassis badly crushed and the engine jammed against the fan belt; we had no choice but to tow the Peugeot the 140 kilometers to Nanyuki.

This meant going up the escarpment, which rose 1,230 meters. We were lucky to have a steel tow-rope; even so the clamps needed constant attention as we bumped over the rocky lava. I marveled at James's self-control and patience. Every few kilometers he was obliged to crawl under the car and readjust the clamp, knowing that only a little farther on he would have to repeat the process.

It took us seven hours to reach Nanyuki. By then it was 9:00 P.M. Next morning I was delighted to learn that the garage had a spare chassis available; even so it was two weeks before I got the Peugeot onto the road again. The accident was annoying, but when I thought what might have happened if I had been driving with Penny in her heavy crate inside my Toyota Land-Cruiser, I could only be very thankful that it had occurred when I was alone in the car.

Anxious to know how Penny had got on in my absence, I chartered a plane and flew back to Naivasha. I found her flourishing; evidently Makedde and the young candidate in residence had looked after her very well.

Sorting through my mail, I came across a cable from England announcing the arrival on the following morning of yet another candidate.

I was not impressed by his credentials. He was only twenty-three, had no idea of what camping in the bush over a long period involved, spoke no Swahili and would therefore be unable to cope with labor problems. In fact, he had already written twice applying for the job, but as I had not encouraged him I was surprised that he should take the risk of a long and expensive journey which would probably be fruitless.

To my surprise, Martin established an instant rapport with Penny. This was satisfactory, but I needed someone with camping and administrative experience who had some mechanical knowledge and was proficient with a rifle. Martin had none of these qualifications, so if I took him on I would need two assistants: himself specifically to help with Penny, and the other to look after the camp. This might well appear to be an extravagance, but it was essential to have an efficient team so that if one of us became ill or went on leave there would be no breakdown.

From among a number of candidates I chose Jock, a middle-aged ex-farmer who loved life in the bush. My next step was to fit the radio collar onto Penny so that she would get used to it while she was still in familiar surroundings. Patrick Hamilton and Dr. Paul Sayer came to help us. Since it was not easy to get the exact measurements of Penny's neck the adjustments would inevitably take some time. Paul therefore sedated Penny, giving her 500 milligrams of Ketalar in two doses with an interval between them. He did this to minimize the danger of over-sedating her. While this was going on Patrick connected the batteries and transmitter which were encapsulated in a solid block of plastic placed between a double layer of the neoprene-impregnated nylon belting of the collar, which was $3\frac{1}{2}$ centimeters wide. He then punched holes in the material, taking into account that as Penny grew he would need to widen the collar. After that he riveted the collar around Penny's neck. While she was sedated Paul took a number of measurements:

From tip of nose to base of skull	25 cm
From skull to base of tail	99 cm
Tail itself	69 cm
Total length	193 cm
Width of neck	43 cm
Girth of heart	72 cm
Permanent left upper canines	25 cm
Permanent left lower canines	21 cm
Weight (with collar)	$35\frac{1}{2}$ kg
Weight of collar	1 kg

Judging by these measurements Penny was probably 12 months old and, because she was a forest leopard from Narok, which lies at an altitude of nearly 2,000 meters, she was already as big as a fully grown Shaba leopard which lived at an altitude of only 1,000 meters; she was also much darker and more beautifully patterned than the low-country leopard.

While Penny was coming to, Patrick showed us how to handle the antenna and the receiver. This worked well enough provided we were not separated from Penny by rocky hills, deep ravines, or trees; if we were, then to take the readings of the signals we needed to get onto high ground, or even onto the roof of the car.

After three hours Penny was still very wobbly and apt to collapse and it was evidently going to take her several more hours to recover fully. As Paul and Patrick now left for Nairobi, and I had to go off to give a lecture at one of the hotels on the Lake, I left Martin in charge, promising him that I would be back by 9:00 P.M.

When I returned I learned that soon after I had left Penny had torn her collar off. Alone with her and in the dark, Martin had had to act quickly while she was still sleepy. He collected a torch and the punching tool and, holding the torch between his teeth, punched one more hole into the hard fabric of the collar and riveted the ends rather more tightly around Penny's neck.

I was most grateful for his efficient handling of the situation, for if he had waited for my return, by which time Penny would have fully recovered consciousness, it would have been impossible to fit the collar without sedating her again.

Now, as I looked at her lying fast asleep, I had mixed feelings about the telemetric device I had wished on her. Patrick had camouflaged the collar by painting spots on it. All the same it looked clumsy, and spoiled Penny's natural beauty. Records of experiments with radio collars appear to prove that they do not irritate the animals, yet I wondered if we had any right to impair their beauty. My only excuse was that the more I learned about the character of leopards, the better I would be able to protect them.

Next morning when we went for our walk Penny did not seem to mind her collar even though the 4-centimeter-thick capsule which contained the batteries dangled below her chin; but it did not prevent her from licking herself without difficulty and crawling with her head pressed to the ground when ambushing us. This was her favorite game; crouching low and quivering with excitement, she made us take great

care to hide behind any cover before her final assault. Most of the time
she kept her claws sheathed, but sometimes she forgot; so we continued
the precaution of always wearing canvas gloves.

About this time I received a letter from a friend in which she suggested that I should compare dog-like cats with cat-like cats. She wrote
that in her opinion the lion was a dog-like cat because it had a straight-
forward look and open character, and needed to share its life with other
lions. Tigers, panthers, and leopards she regarded as cat-like cats, while
a cheetah was hard to classify since it had traits of both species. I agreed
with what she said about lions and had found Penny, with her need to
conceal herself, a different proposition, so perhaps she was a cat-like cat.

When the Peugeot was repaired and delivered to Naivasha, and the
camp at Shaba was ready to receive us, Paul Sayer very kindly arranged
to take time off from his exacting work at the university to accompany
us on our move, which was fixed for August 31.

We planned a small motorcade. First would come Paul's Kombi
Volkswagen, driven by his wife and containing his two children and
Makedde. Next would come my Toyota Land-Cruiser; Paul would
travel in it, and so would Penny in her heavy crate. I would bring up
the rear, driving Martin and the cook in my Peugeot. Paul sedated
Penny with Ketalar, and also gave her an injection of Felidovac against
feline enteritis. The distance we had to cover was 364 kilometers. We
started at 9:00 A.M., and in normal circumstances, even allowing for a
picnic lunch, it should not have taken us more than five or six hours. But
our circumstances were not normal. Paul wished, given the unpredictable reaction of cats to sedatives, to administer only the minimum
dose of Ketalar, and was prepared to give an additional dose if and
when she came to on the way.

Our route took us from Naivasha across the northern Aberdares to the
Thomson Falls, by which time we had climbed to an altitude of 2,300
meters. At this point the road was undergoing major repairs, and recent
rains had turned it into a quagmire. We skidded and slithered through
deep mud and then waited for the others to catch up with us. When
they didn't appear I drove back and found the Kombi with a puncture
and a broken jack. As the Peugeot's jack cannot operate on other cars,
we had to improvise a way of lifting the wheel; that took us two
hours. During this time a storm blew up which made the road very
tricky indeed. By now there was no question of having a picnic, for we
were entirely occupied with keeping the cars on the road.

It was 3:00 P.M. when we reached Nanyuki, where we filled up with gas. News of Penny's journey had already reached the town, and I found myself surrounded by people asking for my autograph, but we had little time for them since our chief concern was to reach the camp before dark. Earlier we had suffered from a road that turned into a quagmire; now, descending 1,230 meters, from Nanyuki via Isiolo to Shaba, we were enveloped by dust. Previously we had been very cold, but now we felt the heat. Penny, though asleep, was panting heavily. In all, the drive took us nine hours, and during it Paul had injected Penny seven times with the sedative—15 cc, or 1,500 mg in all—a very heavy dose and in fact the full amount that he thought safe to give her. Thanks to Paul's skill and care Penny had slept throughout the whole journey and would have no memory of it. The sun was setting and shadows were creeping across the camp when we reached our destination. We carried the leopardess in her crate to her boma.

Then we sat down and opened a bottle of champagne. I had been given it months before and was saving it for a worthy occasion. Surely the opening of this new chapter in my life was a suitable one. For seven years I had been hoping for just such an occasion.

As I looked around me I thought how wonderfully everything had turned out. Within a few yards of me was this lovely creature who would now be free to live her life in ideal country. The Warden was in favor of my project, I had two assistants and a reliable and pleasant staff to help me, the camp was well built, and I could hope that there would be enough money left for me to complete my leopard study. It had taken a long time to arrive at this favorable situation—my one regret was that we had only one bottle of champagne.

By ten o'clock Penny opened her eyes; her gaze was blurred, and she staggered when she got to her feet. We gave her some Farex mixed with milk and glucose, then we all went to bed. My sleeping tent and my study tent were very close to Penny's boma—I would be able to see her at all times. In the stillness of the night, which was only occasionally broken by the crackling of a log in the campfire, I thought how marvelous it was that at last my dream had come true.

At dawn I found Penny still swaying drunkenly in her boma. I gave her some more Farex, milk, and glucose, after which she recovered her balance and watched Makedde and myself as we covered the wooden platforms in the corners of her boma with swamp grass. These platforms would provide her with shade, and we made ladders of logs which would make it easier for her to climb up to them. Within the boma there were two dead trees which we cut to a suitable height so that she could rest in them without being able to escape if she jumped from them. The boma itself was very large, and separated from the camping ground only by wire netting. We had also used the netting to make a roof over the enclosure to prevent predators from climbing in and attacking her.

The contrast between her new home and her old home was very sharp. At Elsamere the climate was ideal and the ground covered with grass; here, the sun was fierce, and the red soil was burned and strewn with lava boulders.

James did his best to clear the campsite of stones, but he could not help with another nuisance: the acacia trees which overshadowed the area, giving welcome shade, but also continuously dropping inch-long thorns. In spite of these minor inconveniences this was the most impressive camp I had lived in in my forty years in Africa. There were comfortable sleeping tents, each with a small verandah and a bathroom annex. There was a tent for me to use as a study, which had plenty of pockets to hold papers and a small cupboard that locked and could be used for papers or money. Next to it was a tent in which we stored our many boxes of food and our camping kit. Besides these five tents there was a large dining tent which contained two refrigerators and many shelves, and a tent with a carpenter's bench and a number of tools. At one end of the camp was a very large tent for the Africans, complete with shower and toilet, and at the opposite end of the camp, a shower and toilet for us.

When digging the 6-meter drops for the toilet the men had struck water. To avoid pollution James had cemented the floors of the toilet. The center of the camp was dominated by a vast kitchen table which might have been the pride of a de luxe hotel. In contrast, a heap of accumulated ash was in fact our cooking stove. Pots were buried in it and heated by burning logs placed over the ash. Of course this method of cooking can only be used in a stationary camp. When we were on safari three small portable stoves had to fulfill the same function. It is remarkable what good food safari cooking can produce by these primitive methods; Kifosha, for instance, baked bread and cakes, made a variety of delicious dishes and even ice cream with the sole assistance of our ash heap.

The staff had an ash heap of their own, similar to ours but a little smaller. It stood close to their tent and opposite a large stone that marked an unknown grave. There are many such cairns in northern Kenya. No one seems to know who made them. Today, as they pass by, most tribesmen honor the memory of the unknown dead by adding a pebble to the pile, and as a result some cairns are by now 2 or 3 meters high and may have a diameter of 8 meters. Our cairn was about this size and, judging by the state of the pebbles, must have been erected a long time ago. To keep the campsite rectangular, we had included the cairn inside the wire even though we knew it would be the home of many scorpions. Perhaps they were guarding the spirit of the dead, for when a laborer sat on the cairn he usually got stung.

The fence around the camp was made of 3-meter-high wire and looked as though it was built to last forever. Our vital asset, the spring, was only 50 meters outside the fence. By using filters we provided ourselves with crystal-clear water; some neighboring trees afforded us a shady garage. Not only did our campsite seem to me to be specially designed for us, but Penny had a thicket to hide in, a playground of soft swamp grass, and plenty of water. While I was inspecting our new home the others went for a game-viewing drive. They returned at 10:00 A.M. and by then Penny was sufficiently recovered to eat about a kilogram of raw meat and drink a lot of milk. Paul examined her and was satisfied that the strong dose of Ketalar had left no ill effects. He gave us a generous supply of medications in case of emergency and then left. Paul had, in the past as well as in the present, done much more for our animals than we could possibly have expected of him. I was deeply grateful to him, and when he and his delightful family departed, I felt sure that our friendship had deepened.

Soon afterwards the Assistant Warden came to welcome us. Hussein was a young Somali who had only recently completed a course in wildlife management. He was keen to prove himself, and offered us his help. Duly impressed by Penny, he watched her, but from a distance, because, after all, "a leopard is a leopard."

CHAPTER FOUR

Exploring
the New Surroundings

WHILE IN NANYUKI I had been given the shoulder and front leg of a calf which had died of a non-infectious disease. Hoping to break Penny of her habit of eating only small pieces of meat I gave her this joint. By next morning she still had not touched it. We took her for a walk and when we went home for lunch we left her on lava ground where there were nonetheless plenty of trees which would provide shelter for her siesta. When we returned there was no sign of her so we followed the bleeping of the radio signal for a while, and after crossing the spoor of many baboons we found Penny in a new area, tucked under a thick bush. When we walked toward the camp she followed us but constantly looked behind her. Finally she went back a short distance as though waiting for some-one. Makedde told us that a few days ago he had found fresh leopard spoor near this place. We searched the area but found no trace of any leopard.

When we reached camp Penny had caught up with us and I offered her the calf leg again; she took it to her platform but only licked it. She had not drunk her milk and so, hoping that she might become hungry, we locked her into the boma. This infuriated her; she scratched at the door and then paced up and down the wire fence. I managed to force three little pieces of meat into her mouth through the wire; then I opened the door.

Instantly she vanished into the darkness. We went after her with a spotlight but all we could see were the green reflections of the eyes of a herd of waterbuck.

Before dawn we heard the sound of large animals stampeding close to the camp and when daylight came we discovered the spoor of oryx. They had obviously been chased either by a large leopard or by a lioness.

We spotted Penny up a tree some hundred meters away. She was very happy and unwilling to come down; although she must have been hungry it took us half an hour to get her to descend and eat small pieces of meat and drink a little milk. Her coat, usually so silky, was very sticky, especially around her ears. This suggested that some animal had licked her. There was mud on her radio collar.

Yawning, she moved into a thorny thicket under the tree on which we had found her; crawling after her, I offered her some meat. Reluctantly she took three small pieces and that only as if to please me; then she turned her head and I was dismissed. The time was 7:30 A.M. As a rule she was at her most active at this hour, so I wondered whether she could possibly have found a mate. She was now 13 months old, and this was usually the time for the onset of puberty. Later we found her by the thicket overlooking the swamp. She was being watched by the eleven buffalo who were nearly always around the camp.

Too tired even to play, Penny appeared to be waiting for someone. Slowly and reluctantly she followed us to the boma. Here she again refused the calf leg but hungrily devoured some chopped camel meat mixed with milk. After finishing this meal she carried the leg toward the thicket. It was by then too dark for me to see what she did with it.

At six o'clock next morning I was awakened by the yapping of some jackals behind the camp. Later we found Penny in the area where, the night before, I had seen her disappear with the calf leg. We searched the place thoroughly and could see no sign of the meat, but we saw three jackals scampering toward the swamp.

Penny then moved toward one end of the thicket and settled down for her midday sleep. This thicket was about 100 meters wide and 400 long and consisted of almost impenetrable bush, so it was not going to be easy to find a calf leg in it. Nevertheless I was determined to discover if at least some bones had remained. I sent Makedde to search the far side while I combed the near side.

As often happens in the bush, one goes out to look for a certain thing, but failing to find it discovers something much more exciting: so now

Makedde returned, grinning, to report a fresh Grant's gazelle kill. It was only 150 meters from the staff quarters. Makedde added that at dawn he had seen Penny, followed by three jackals, coming from this direction. We went to investigate and found the ground patterned with the spoor of a leopard and several jackals. They led toward the camp.

The stomach of the carcass was uneaten and indeed the rest was untouched except for scratches on the neck and shoulders which could only have been made by the razor-sharp claws of a leopard.

I was puzzled—it was a very large buck for Penny to have tackled for her first kill. If, however, she had done so, why had she not defended it from the jackals instead of leaving it unprotected while leading us to the thicket? The previous evening she had had a large meal of camel meat after which she had carried the leg into the thicket. Was it not odd then that she should have left it and gone off to hunt a gazelle? It was also strange that there was no trace of blood on her. If, on the other hand, a wild leopard had been responsible for the kill, why had he not guarded it from the jackals or at least stored it up some tree where they could not get at it? Of course it was possible that the killer had been the leopard that Makedde had seen at dawn and that, finding himself observed, he had gone off.

Hoping to learn more from Penny's reactions, we returned to the place where we had found the Grant, after taking her for her afternoon walk. All afternoon Penny had been very sleepy and it had taken a lot of rabbit skin wriggling to induce her to follow us to the place of the kill.

When we were within 20 meters of it we stood still, expecting her to lead us to the carcass or alternatively to prevent us from approaching it. But she walked along as though she did not know that there was a kill nearby. Eventually we led her to the carcass. When she saw it she seemed frightened and hopped away, only to return and tap the shoulder cautiously and then pounce on it, tearing frantically at the skin. She made no attempt to drag the kill away and indeed seemed as puzzled by it as we were by her behavior. Soon she settled down close by and seemed bored with the whole affair.

When Martin and I succeeded in enticing Penny to play on a fallen tree, Makedde removed the buck to the boma, to protect it from scavengers. Later Penny rolled happily on buffalo pats and drank at the swamp; she certainly did not react as though it was her kill.

We thought perhaps that during the night she would eat some of the carcass or that if it were the kill of a wild leopard he might return, attracted by its scent, in which case we should find his spoor close to the boma. But in the morning there were no new leopard spoors to be seen and Penny had not touched the carcass, even though, judging by the way she wolfed down the camel meat, she must have been very hungry. For the next few days she only moved between the camp, the swamp, and this thicket where she spent the night.

Many scientists deny that animals can reason. I do not agree. Indeed, I think that Penny is gifted with a sense of humor as well as reason. Take the day when Martin put the rabbit skin very high up on a tree but left the chain to which it was attached dangling down and well within her reach. Penny, having observed this, at once pulled the handle of the chain, thus getting hold of the skin without having to exert herself. She then looked straight at Martin with what could only be described as a broad grin. After this, pulling the chain became one of her favorite games and the more we laughed the more she enjoyed it.

Like Elsa and Pippa, Penny hated being photographed. I thought this might be because when we take a picture we look in a detached way at our model, and no doubt our expression is different from the one we have when we are communicating, talking, and looking at our subject. I believe that animals are more sensitive to this change in attitude than people are. Animals either move away or turn their heads. Because of this reaction, if we wanted Penny to go on walking, with the rabbit skin to entice her, we only had to focus a camera on her to set her in motion.

When George was Game Warden of Kenya's Northern Frontier Province we were often far from civilization for months on end and did not see anyone except our staff. Life in the bush is timeless and because I had so many interests to occupy my mind I was often unaware which month it was, not to mention which day of the week—for to me every day was Sunday—at least this was my idea of a holy day. Now, however, since I was responsible for everyone in the camp I had to devise something to break up the weekly routine, for if I did not there would be a risk that the men would find the loneliness of this remote place unbearable.

We were lucky that there was a lovely waterfall 10 kilometers from camp, where the spring emptied its crystal water into the Uaso Nyiro torrent before it reached the crocodile-infested river. Here there was a pool contained by a natural dam. To reach it we had to scramble over the nearly perpendicular cliff. When we got there we found a sandy beach. The men were able to bathe in the pool and fish. Meanwhile I stood under the cascade, which provided me with a good massage treatment. This became our Sunday treat, but since fishing was not one of my hobbies—nor did I feel a constant need for massage—I sometimes stayed in camp.

As I watched the fishermen go off it seemed unfair that Makedde and the cook should be armed only with improvised rods made of the rib of a palm frond to which was attached a line cobbled out of twine, while Jock and Martin had very sophisticated tackle. Yet on their return it was often Makedde and Kifosha who had caught delicious barbels while the other two had no fish and had often lost hook after hook.

One evening while we were sitting in the open after supper there was a commotion outside the camp. In the beam of our flashlight we saw the eyes of some thirty goats reflecting greenly, and a Somali armed with a spear. When we asked him what he was doing at this late hour in a Game Reserve he muttered that he had got lost in the dark and, seeing our lights, believed he was approaching a Somali *manyatta*. This was an obvious lie, for the border was far away and he must have crossed it in the morning to reach our camp by evening with his slow-moving goats. Also he must have known that for a year Shaba had been closed to human settlement. Since there were border problems at the moment between Somalia and Kenya, and as we knew that Somali guerrillas were within 30 kilometers of the Park's border, we listened to his story with some reservations. Just as we were discussing what to do, Penny appeared. So far as we knew she had never before been near a herd of animals. She wriggled close to the ground along the fence and looked as if she were ready to charge the goats. I asked Makedde to confiscate the man's spear in case he might hurl it at Penny, after which we were obliged to give him and his goats hospitality for the night inside the camp.

Later we decided that at crack of dawn Jock should drive to the Shaba gate and collect a few Rangers to arrest the Somali. He left before dawn but by the time the rest of us woke the Somali and his goats had vanished. We looked for Penny, whom we found hiding in the thicket. All our efforts to make her join us were wasted and we were puzzled until we noticed two Game Rangers tracking after the goat spoors. Penny must have sensed their presence long before we saw them; it was for this reason that she did not budge. I was glad that she was frightened of strangers and that she only allowed Martin and me to be friendly with her, while tolerating Jock and Makedde at a distance. If we could keep our pride restricted to the four of us she would have no association with other human beings and when we withdrew she would be able to revert quickly to living completely wild.

Hoping to encourage her to hunt during the night, we reversed our feeding schedule by giving her her big meal after our morning walk so that she could digest it during the day when she was sleepy. In the evenings we fed her only tidbits in order to keep her hungry after dark.

Unfortunately, now that she had discovered the thicket near the camp she seldom moved out of its labyrinth. Each day she chose a different place, possibly to make it difficult for us to find her. Elsa and Pippa had always responded to our calls with a low purr, but Penny would allow us to pass within a meter without making a sound. Even when we knew she was close we could often not detect her whereabouts unless we used the telemetric device.

Plainly she felt very safe in the thicket even when on at least one occasion lions were prowling close to it. It puzzled me that she did not realize that she was much more vulnerable to predators in this hideout than she would have been on the branch of a tree. To try to break her of the habit, one morning we coaxed her to follow us up the elephant lugga until we reached a gorge which led into a narrow path between the cliffs. Here Penny discovered some small caves. Judging by the large bones of antelope which we found inside them, they had been occupied by hyenas; some quills suggested that a porcupine had also lived here.

As I watched Penny hopping swiftly across the rocks and investigating all the cracks and crevices, I realized how essential rocks are to a leopard's well-being. A new game which we now played with her was to throw the rabbit skin up the cliff into some inaccessible spot. Penny would watch us with great concentration, then jump effortlessly up the perpendicular wall, after which she slipped like a shadow along any ledges that gave her foothold. When she reached the skin she would pick it up and make her way back to give it to us; then the game would be repeated interminably.

Here Penny was in her element, but Martin, in his effort to place the skin in a difficult position, had to scramble up rocks that a leopard could climb easily but which were dangerous for a man to tackle. Penny would watch his movements with keen interest and sometimes—as if to tease him—instead of bringing the skin back to us she would carry it into a cave, usually one concealed by thorny bushes through which Martin had to scramble; then, when he was making his perilous way down, Penny would close in behind him and nip his bottom. I did not envy Martin this sport but it seemed that he as well as Penny enjoyed it, for it went on until the heat was great and Penny retired into the cave. Hoping that she might remain there, we sneaked off; but though she liked her new playground she did not mean to be left alone in a new area, so, before long, we saw her tracking behind us along the lugga until she reached her thicket. I was quite determined to widen her territory, and in the afternoon, though she was still tired from her exertions, I managed to move her to the swamp.

We spent a relaxing afternoon there, Penny rolling on her back inviting us to stroke her and, when I did so, closing her eyes in bliss. It was a very peaceful scene: the leopard lying between us while we watched a herd of Grant's gazelles, an ostrich, four zebras, and our friends the buffaloes grazing under the bluest of skies.

It seemed to me that this was a golden opportunity for measuring Penny, now almost 14 months old. Luckily, I found a string in my pocket long enough to serve as a tape measure. While I was concentrating on getting accurate measurements from the tip of her nose to the end of her tail, I did not notice that the buffaloes had approached to within 50 meters and were sniffing our scent. Suddenly Penny sat up and was off like a shot. We followed her and saw the buffaloes swerve in the other direction.

Of course this would have to happen on the one day our good guardian Makedde was in Isiolo. I believe that buffalo in a herd are nothing like as dangerous as a single buffalo, but Penny was scared and afterwards would not leave the thicket. Next morning she still refused to come out. To give her moral support and also to have an opportunity to sketch her, I crawled with all my paraphernalia into the thicket.

I found her at the far end in a well-shaded hollow. She watched me suspiciously as I cleared a space free of thorns to sit down on. When I unfolded my sketching material this was too much for her. I had only time to rise to my feet before she pounced on me. To protect myself against her claws and not having much space to move in, I poured the water I had brought for my painting over Penny. This diverted her attention and she retreated into her hideout and settled down. I stuck it out for three hours and then left.

Next morning we found her stretched out on the branch of a tree. We had brought the same water can we used to bring to Elsa and Pippa. Penny was so thirsty that she could not wait for us to pour the water out and licked the can. Although she had lost a lot of weight since we came to Shaba and had not eaten for twenty-four hours, she would not touch the meat we brought.

At 9:00 A.M. we returned to camp, leaving water and her daily ration of meat. She had had an exhausting game with Martin and seemed sleepy. On our return at tea time we found the meat untouched. Nevertheless, after she had drunk she was full of energy and Martin was kept on his toes playing hide-and-seek with her.

When it got dark Penny accompanied us to the entrance of the gorge, for all the world as though she were a good hostess taking leave of her guests at the front door. Of course she may instead have been making sure that we were really going away and not preparing to spy on her nightly activities.

For the next seven days she made the gorge her home. We often found her stretched out on the branch of a tree just outside the ravine where she must have been cool.

A jackal came nightly to quench his thirst at Penny's water trough. Perhaps he thought it safer to drink when protected by wire than from the swamp. Every night I heard him lapping and every morning saw his spoor, till one night the lapping had a different sound. I switched on my torch and saw Penny at the trough. I was delighted, because lately I had noticed that her radio collar was getting rather tight and had been worried about how I would be able to loosen it in the bush. Now, since she had returned to camp, I thought we had only to keep her thirsty for her to return during the midday heat so that we could adjust her collar without sedating her. However, as though aware of my plan, next morning nothing would induce her to enter the boma and she went to the swamp to drink before retreating to her thicket.

In the afternoon we took her for an unusually long walk away from the swamp. As she trotted after us she panted heavily and I felt like a brute, but when we got home she entered the boma and had a long drink. As she was so exhausted by the heat and the exercise, she never noticed when we followed her and shut the door. When she discovered she was a prisoner, she was furious. All night she paced up and down the wire and we even heard her scratching at the fence, trying to dig herself out. Luckily the wire was buried to a depth of 1 foot. This defeated her but did not improve her temper. When at daybreak I joined her she made it plain that I was in disgrace. I tried to calm her with affectionate words but she only increased the pace of her runs up and down the fence, refused meat and milk, and ignored me. I was obliged to keep her shut up till midday, when it became too hot for her. Then she went to sleep and we chose this moment to adjust her collar, which we succeeded in doing without waking her up.

From now onwards Penny avoided the camp and stayed close to the thicket. When we wished to take her for a walk she only followed for a short distance. On the third night after she had left the boma, we heard lions close by and in the morning saw their pug marks all around the fence. This made me realize that Penny must have sensed their approach long before we were aware of it and had taken her precautions.

We know that animals have senses in many cases more developed than our own; of course I have no accurate knowledge of the acuteness of hearing of a leopard, but I do know that lions can hear sounds coming from twice as far away as a human ear can register them.

The incident which taught me this took place near Lake Naivasha, which stretches 13 kilometers from the border of our garden to the opposite shore. Here friends of ours kept two tame lions. This was the time when Boy, the lion who had played a part in the film *Born Free*, was staying at Elsamere, recovering from a severe wound inflicted by a buffalo. The two lions on the other shore roared incessantly, to the surprise of their owner, for till then they had been pretty quiet. We, for our part, were bewildered because Boy stared constantly across the lake, seemed very agitated, and roared for all he was worth. All efforts to calm him proved useless. The explanation came from friends who had been in the middle of the lake fishing that weekend. They had heard a lively lion duet coming from both sides of the water, but the people on either shore heard no sound coming from the opposite bank. This surely proves that lions have far better hearing than we have.

In addition to her superior hearing Penny appeared to have senses that we know nothing about which warned her of approaching danger. We concluded that if we watched her carefully we would have a good chance of keeping out of trouble.

CHAPTER FIVE

Bush Life

PENNY WAS NOW 15 months old and ready to take an interest in a male leopard—but where was she to find one? By now we had covered all of our exercise ground without having seen the spoor of any leopard. We had been told that leopards lived in the mountains outside the Shaba Reserve, but these were too far away and Penny had no chance of meeting them. While we were considering this problem Ken Smith was staying with us; readers of *Born Free* will remember that he was with George on the day they collected the three orphaned cubs, one of whom became Elsa. Ken was now in charge of the development of new Game Reserves including, of course, Shaba.

We consulted him about our problem. He suggested that we should translocate a cattle-raiding leopard from a farming area and release it in Penny's neighborhood.

The plan sounded simple but translocation is in fact a complicated operation for which much preparatory study is needed if one hopes to avoid the mistakes that have occurred in previous experiments of this type. For instance, during the last ten years ninety cattle-raiding leopards have been caught and released in the Meru Reserve where they have disappeared so completely that no one knows if they have survived.

Today Patrick Hamilton is engaged in a two-year research project to discover the movements of translocated and resident leopards—at least of those that have been equipped with radio collars.

A wild animal that has been trapped and translocated becomes very upset and has been known to go berserk the moment it is released from its traveling crate. Moreover, because the homing instinct in leopards is particularly strong, moving them is a risky experiment. All the cat species have this homing instinct, but it seems to be more strongly developed in leopards than in any of the others. Indeed, many leopards are known to have set off on their way back to their old home the moment they were released. In some cases they have traveled great distances before reaching it.

All in all, I thought that the chances of a translocated leopard settling down in Shaba were slim, but if we were to try it out I believed that the best hope would be to keep the new arrival confined and well-fed for just as long as it took for him to recover from the trauma of being trapped and moved. How long he would have to remain confined we would only be able to discover by trial and error.

After much thought, we decided that Ken should ask the government for permission for us to provide a mate for Penny. Meanwhile we would build a boma for our hoped-for guest. It would have to be at a safe distance from the camp so that the formerly cattle-raiding leopard would not get accustomed to human activities, but it would also have to be near enough to make it possible for us to provide meat and water daily.

Knowing how long the government's reply was likely to take to reach us, I wrote to several farmers who had recently got rid of cattle-raiding leopards, asking for help in providing a male. I also ordered another radio collar from the States. Meanwhile the bride-to-be was unaware of the problems she had raised. She was now venturing into a new area some 1½ kilometers from camp. We found her there, hiding in a dense thorn bush which was part of the bush belt that divided a lava slope from the limestone acacia-covered plain.

She did not come to meet us, seemed unwilling to take the usual morning walk, and when we offered her water she got up and I noticed that her belly was full. She drank thirstily and gulped several times, something she had never done till now. This made us search for the remains of a kill but we didn't find even a bird's feather, much less the remains of a dik-dik. When we left her to return home, Penny did not leave her hideout though she watched us disappear. This was the first time she had chosen to make a home in an unfamiliar area. Next morning she was still there and was very thirsty. After drinking her fill she followed us for a kilometer to the end of the swamp, the place we called "Lion Corner" because it was there that, soon after our arrival at Shaba, we had seen the five lions. Today we watched two striped jackals playing around. They saw us but seemed unconcerned for they went on rolling over each other and biting each other's tails. For half an hour they chased around, coming quite near to Penny, who had hidden herself not far from us in a bush.

When it began to get dark we started to make our way home. Suddenly a small herd of buffalo emerged from the reeds surrounding the swamp and we nearly collided with them.

In the morning Penny was back at her favorite thorn bush; nearby was the fresh spoor of lions and jackals. She ate her meal and drank a lot but was reluctant to come for a walk with us. I could understand why she preferred the limestone plain, full of Grant's gazelles, dik-dik, jackals, and hares, not to mention birds, to the lava gorge where there was little prey.

For the next week, while consenting to come with us on our walks on the plain, she returned every evening to her thicket. It was obvious that in the future this was going to be her H.Q. Here she would have access to water and there would be enough prey around to keep her from hunger. But for the moment, in the hope of helping her to become familiar with the wide range of her possible hunting ground, we carried food and water to her wherever she chose to be.

While exploring the vast limestone plain, we encouraged Penny to stalk any animals that were about. She was interested but never made an effort to chase any of them, let alone to make a kill. Sometimes she would cautiously approach the bush and sniff around it, but if a bird emerged she made no attempt to catch it and just watched it fly off. The Grant's gazelles interested her, but only so long as they were at a safe distance. Keeping close to us she would stalk them, crouching stealthily forward, her belly to the ground and using any possible cover, while also keeping an eye on us. If we stopped she stopped too. It seemed as though she were leaving us the initiative to make the final rush.

Sometimes I lost patience and whispered, "Go, Penny, go" and pushed her forward and even poked at her, hoping to induce her to move, but she just looked questioningly at me, then sank down onto the grass.

One day we maneuvered her toward a jackal; when only about 20 meters from him she did make a rush. A second later both animals had disappeared behind a bush. From the alarmed yapping of the jackal we assumed that Penny was holding him down, then from some distance came the call of another jackal; we thought it was replying to distress signals from one of the pack. Soon Penny and her potential prey appeared from behind the bush. The jackal did not seem to be in any way injured and trotted off to meet his friend. Penny flung herself down, exhausted, at my feet. Later when the two jackals appeared and approached her while she was playing with Martin, she ignored them.

This incident happened near the bush where a week earlier we had seen Penny and which had now become her feeding place. Makedde named it "Hoteli," because whenever we offered water and meat to her she passed all the other shady bushes and however tired she might be dragged herself to this one.

Like all animals she was very conservative in her habits and once she had decided that a place was right for resting, playing, or feeding she would stick to it. Some scientists attribute such animal behavior to conditioned reflexes and release mechanisms. Certainly we human beings behave in the same way, so are we also dependent on them? Watch on which chair a new guest settles and next time he comes you may be sure that unless it is already occupied he will again sit in it. Don't you find yourself also acting in the same way when you visit other people's houses? Possibly this behavior derives from an instinct to establish a territory, for it is evident that anything familiar gives us a sense of security and triggers off a protective memory. The same instinct makes both man and animals avoid places that remind them of a disagreeable experience.

The radio I had ordered and waited so long to receive now arrived. In such a remote place as Shaba we needed a radio to enable us to communicate with the outside world should any emergency arise. George had one at his camp at Kora and I had one at Elsamere, but Mount Kenya, which rises to over 5,000 meters, stands between them and makes reception poor. At Shaba we were only 105 kilometers apart and as there were no mountains to block the waves we would be able to hear each other very clearly. In the past I had often been anxious, wondering how George at seventy-two could cope with fifteen lions, but since driving through his camp on bad roads took a whole day and flying was too expensive, we were often out of touch for quite a time. It was reassuring that with the radios we could now talk at prearranged times and learn what was going on in both our camps.

In November the rains started and there were some very heavy showers. These were welcome to the parched ground and dormant vegetation, but they turned the Park into a quagmire and we had to live in gumboots and thick clothes.

Penny, on the other hand, became much more active. Up to now, she had begun to tire by 8:00 A.M.; but once the rains started, she was ready at that time to go on walking for another couple of hours. When Martin was on leave I became the target for her games, during which in an effort to knock me down she would leap at me with her forelegs outstretched. I protected myself as best I could with canvas gloves and apron, but seeing her so happy and full of energy, I was prepared to put up with some minor scratches, for Penny had missed so much of the normal fun and education of a leopard cub.

She had not had a mother to be her constant companion, to communicate bush lore to her and to teach her how to keep out of danger, particularly during the hours of darkness. This made me realize how important it had been that at Elsamere she had spent her nights alone, for now at Shaba she took it for granted that I would not be with her and seemed to have coped successfully with any nocturnal adventures that had befallen her.

When the rains came Penny's thicket soon grew soggy. She then found herself a retreat in a grove of spiky balanites trees which grew on the lava-strewn slope. Here the water drained off quickly, and the dense undergrowth provided shade. The balanites trees are interesting; they are typical of low altitudes and arid country. If there are giraffes about, they prune the foliage as high as they can reach, and after their departure the trees are shaped like mushrooms. The flowers and leaves are insignificant, but the 2-inch-long thorns that grow in profusion along the branches are formidable.

Many years ago I was making a painting of the balanites when a Swiss author wrote to me asking for a photograph of the tree to use as a frontispiece for his book on Theophrastos, a Greek philosopher and scientist who studied medicinal herbs and was particularly interested in the balanites. It was an extraordinary coincidence that this request should have arrived at the moment at which I was engaged in painting such a tree.

Penny's new lair, which was at some distance from the camp, opened up further territory for our walks. It was situated at the base of a large lava flow which stretched far beyond the camp's boundaries. Luckily the ground was crisscrossed by animal tracks, and these were filled with small chips of lava which made walking easy, at least by comparison with the large overlapping loose boulders.

She, of course, easily outran us, and made the most of her capacity for ambushing. There were a few termite hills in the area; Penny ran around them, chasing the rabbit skin which we, standing on the top of the elevation, flung around in a circle.

It was interesting to see how Penny did her utmost to adapt the games to Martin's and my respective abilities. For instance, when she wanted him to sit down and pat her, she would fling herself at his feet and start nibbling at his jeans. But she knew that if she did this to me I would walk off immediately, for I was bound to be slightly scratched and any scratch made me bleed. So, with me, she just stood up, blocking my way until I stroked her, talked to her in a low, affectionate voice, and picked off any ticks that were troubling her. She loved it when I rubbed her in an effort to groom away the dead hair and keep her coat in good condition.

So far Penny had been fed mainly on small pieces of camel meat mixed with bone meal. Now, to prepare her for dealing with a kill, we drained the blood of a goat and placed it with the liver, lungs, heart, spleen, and tripe in a basin which we presented to her. She sniffed at it, and afterwards carried each piece into her thicket, where she left it un-eaten. As I did not want the meal to be wasted, I collected it and hand-fed it to her.

Next, to put her to the test, I presented her with a whole shoulder of goat. It ended up inside a thorny thicket from which Penny immediately walked away. I spent the best part of the day observing her to see whether she would retrieve and eat it. As she did nothing of the sort, I finally collected it, not wishing to keep open house for jackals.

During one of our walks Penny pulled off her radio collar. Luckily I was very close to her and so was able to put it back around her neck before she had even noticed its loss. The incident made me realize how dependent my leopard research project was on this mechanical device, which was often our only means of locating Penny.

On lava territory it was impossible to trace her spoor. Since the rains had come, the grass was knee-high and the myriad white flowers of the heliotrope covered the bush, turning it into what seemed to be a very beautiful snowfield. Unfortunately, in this lush vegetation all tracks were covered. Covered, too, was the wobbly, uneven terrain, in many places waterlogged, which meant that I had to move very cautiously to avoid falling and breaking a bone or damaging my implanted steel hip.

I now took to carrying a stick not only to help me across uneven ground but also to ward off Penny when she jumped at me. She seemed to regard the sticks, which not only I, but also Martin carried, as new toys. They provided her with something to gnaw against her growing molars. Holding the wood between her paws, she would chew it to splinters unless I was able to wriggle it out of her mouth in time. If I did this, she pounced on me; and if she captured the trophy, she carried it off. Of course she expected me to try to get it back, and this provided her with a new game—not one I liked very much, for not only was I deprived of my support, but this encouraged her to jump at me and I had nothing with which to counter her attacks. Luckily Penny never jumped at Makedde, so by staying between the leopardess and myself he acted as a buffer. Penny resented this, but soon discovered that she had met her match in Makedde, who outwitted all her efforts to get past him. Sometimes, to give herself time to think up a new tactic, she would pretend to sniff at the grass or go chasing a grasshopper.

I knew that with the onset of the rains snakes usually appear; I was therefore surprised that up to now we had never seen one. Then, one morning, we found a 4-foot cobra in the storage tent. After this I began to worry about how Penny, who took a great interest in lizards, would react when she discovered a snake.

Since the rains had started she often rolled in the mud and afterwards licked herself. Elsa and Pippa and their families had all done this, and it made me wonder whether the mud contained some vital mineral that they needed.

One afternoon we heard the long-drawn howl of a jackal. It came from far away, but Penny rushed toward me, apparently terrified, and kept close until we reached her balanites grove. This made me realize that though she was now capable of living on her own for most of the time, she still, when frightened, seemed dependent on me for protection.

During the next few days she moved from the limestone plain toward a little hill described on the map as Turkana Hill. To reach it we had to bypass the swamp, which took us through dense bush for about 2 kilometers. This was a favorite lie-up for buffaloes. When, in the morning, we looked for Penny she hid from us and made it clear that she did not want us to come near her. Next day we found her in even thicker bush from which she emerged only for a quick meal and then vanished. Makedde told us that this was not a good place for Penny to stay in since it was frequented by baboons who might be a danger to her. We tried to coax her back to camp, but she only came halfway, and next day was back in the dense bush.

We did not know what could have attracted Penny to this place, but later we found the answer in the spoor of a leopard who was obviously much larger than she and had come from Turkana Hill. I was afraid the pug marks might have been made by a leopardess, but Makedde assured me that no female would have tolerated Penny in her territory, so I felt very relieved.

From my experience with Elsa and Pippa I knew that sexual play begins at puberty, that is to say, when lions are about 2 years old and cheetahs 17 months, though neither can conceive until later. Not wishing to frighten the male leopard away, next day I refrained from touching Penny although she twice sat at my feet, plainly asking to be patted. Bewildered by my unresponsiveness, she followed us for a short distance as we walked toward camp, but then seemed to decide that if it were a choice between me and her own kind she would choose the leopard even though she was still dependent on my feeding and protecting her.

In the morning we found her still in the same area; she emerged from the bush only to eat and then to disappear. When I searched for the spoor of her wild friend she blocked my way and asked to be patted. I obliged while she rubbed herself affectionately against me; then she jumped at me as though to say, "Now leave me alone please," and quickly disappeared. For two days we had found no spoor of her leopard and so assumed that he had left the area.

During this time we climbed up to Turkana Hill with Penny. She seemed fascinated by the vast view across the surrounding plains and kept on taking her bearings as she moved from boulder to boulder. Later she followed us to the base of the hill and remained there. When we next visited her she refused meat except for a rat which we had trapped in camp. Again she was very friendly, asking to be patted, then suddenly, without the slightest provocation, she jumped at me and tore a deep, 2-inch-long gash in my wrist, next to the artery. I pressed my right hand against the wound, which was bleeding profusely, and walked the 2 kilometers back to camp where I disinfected and dressed it. I got back just before a downpour which lasted all night and flooded the country. Since the wound had not stopped bleeding we decided next morning to drive the 30 kilometers to the nearest Mission hospital to have my wrist stitched up. But after slithering through mud for a short distance we were obliged to return. The rain never stopped, and the morass got deeper.

We wondered how Penny was coping with the situation, so we put on our gumboots and went out to provide her with meat. We found her in a quagmire, bedraggled and unhappy. She bolted the meat we had brought her, did not follow us back to the higher ground, and stayed in the bog. But after another day of heavy rain, she had had enough of it

Penny at Elsamere, three months old

Penny with Joy, four months old

She had a liking for Charles

Penny enjoys being fed, five months old

Resting after a meal, six and a half months old

Penny's favorite platform

Must you carry me?

Penny, six and a half months old

The Colobus monkeys at Elsamere tease Penny mercilessly

First meeting with Makedde, eight months and three weeks old

Retrieving a rabbit skin

Changing moods

Weaver birds' nests

and accompanied us uphill to the lava-strewn hinterland by the camp. There she settled in a nearby tree, but could not be induced to enter her boma. In the morning I got no signal from the radio collar, so I hoped that I could contact Penny by calling her, but the only answer to my call were lions roaring from the direction of Turkana Hill. Penny had obviously sensed their approach long before we suspected it, and this had induced her to leave the area. I grew hoarse from calling without any result, and on the following day still had no luck. I returned, defeated, to the camp where, to my surprise, I found Dick Thomsett and two friends who had come to film Penny.

Up to now I had guarded Penny from press reporters and film producers, but in the case of Dick Thomsett, who was making a film of my life and needed a scene with Penny to round it off, I was prepared to make an exception. Now we had to find Penny.

We found her in a dense, thorny thicket from where she was able to overlook the rain pool which, judging by the many spoors surrounding it, must have been visited by a great variety of animals—in particular by wart hogs.

It was no easy job to induce her to emerge from her fortress as she was obviously puzzled not only by Dick Thomsett's presence, but also by his large movie camera. Luckily her curiosity soon made her wish to examine the new toy and she prodded Dick's legs as she tried to get hold of it. He had to invent all sorts of devices to maintain sufficient distance between Penny and his camera to film her. It needed a lot of skill and patience to get a few scenes of Penny drinking at the pool, stretching her tendons on the bole of a tree, retrieving a rag from a bush, and being hand-fed by me. Dick soon realized that filming a leopard was even more tricky than coping with the most capricious woman star. Luckily the rain stopped long enough for our filming session, so he and his friends could leave.

Penny then went back to Turkana Hill, although we found the pug marks of five lions nearby. But at least this was the only place where she would never get bogged down, no matter how much it rained, for the hill was a quartz outcrop. It was a good place for her as she could survey the plain below and spot any approaching danger; besides, there were enough lizards, mice, and birds for her to hunt, and, since the hill was only 2 kilometers from camp, it was easy for us to walk there twice a day to help her with food. Of course when the ground was dry we went there by car. She remained at Turkana Hill for twelve days, the longest time she had yet spent in one area. After this she led us to the limestone plain and went much farther than her old "Hoteli" thicket until she reached a cluster of thorny bushes.

For the next three days Penny stayed put, after which she followed us reluctantly in the direction of the "Hoteli" but keeping a long way behind us. Suddenly we saw a jackal stalking her; instead of charging him, she bolted while he chased her toward us. He stopped only when he saw us and even then he went on yapping at her. After this she kept close to me and we walked on for another hour, until we reached the swamp. By then the sun was setting and the whole country was glowing warmly. Suddenly Makedde gripped my shoulder and pointed toward an aardwolf some hundred meters away; he had his back to us and was cleaning himself. We sank into the long grass and kept still. This was the first time in my forty years in Kenya that I had seen this wonderful nocturnal creature in the wild. I watched it, fascinated. He looked rather like a striped hyena though he was smaller, more elegantly proportioned, and his light sandy coat contrasted strikingly with the black vertical stripes on his body; his mane reached from his head to the root of his tail and made him look larger than he was. I was entranced by his sheer beauty.

Penny seemed to wish to stalk him; the wind was in our favor, and the aardwolf was unaware of our presence. Wriggling herself forward, her body close to the ground, the leopardess came very close to the aardwolf and then gave him a loud, sound slap. Without a backward glance, he ran for his life. Penny, apparently bewildered, stood still and then looked back at us as though to ask, "What next?" Meanwhile four jackals had appeared and one made straight for Penny, who was still watching the disappearing aardwolf. When she heard the jackal barking a challenge, it was her turn to bolt, with the jackal close on her heels. The light was fading, so, knowing that the jackals could not harm Penny, we left.

It seemed incredible to me that she had fearlessly stalked the aardwolf, who could have been a formidable opponent, but was afraid of a jackal, to which she was physically much superior. I thought she must by now be the laughing stock of the local jackals, unless, of course, they had only intended to play with her.

A jackal is a very friendly creature. Had the species not been rabies-carriers, they would surely have ended up as pets. We had often watched them playing hide-and-seek with Pippin, my cairn terrier, and once we had even seen one playing with Elsa, the lioness.

Makedde had said that there must be a gentleman's agreement among all predators not to hurt jackals. This seems to be borne out by the fact that we had seen a jackal sneak up to a lion's kill while the great beast was still eating his meal, and he was not chased off.

Perhaps it was because Penny had never had a four-legged playmate that she mistook the jackal's invitation for a charge. We had noticed that she had made the same mistake with the Grant's gazelles and gerenuk which we sometimes met grazing in the bush. Often she would have had good cover to stalk them but she seemed afraid and remained close to us.

Lately she had become quite efficient at killing birds and frogs, whose presence she sensed at a distance of up to 10 meters. She killed them and ate them at once without even pausing on her walk. Yet she had never attempted to chase, let alone kill, a hare. Hoping to stimulate her hunting instinct, we wriggled a dead rabbit on a string in front of her. She just chased it and picked it up, then ran off proudly with it, but only to store it in a thicket. Up to now she had only been fed on skinned rabbit and as I've said, even when at Elsamere, she had often stored part of her meal on one of the platforms in her boma. It now struck me that this habit might be so imprinted on her that, even though her killing instinct had not yet been awakened (except in the case of birds and frogs), she still kept to her old behavior; that of a very provident house-keeper. It took a long time before we could induce her to eat the skins of the dead rabbits we supplied her with.

Patrick Hamilton told me that, at Tsavo, his leopards lived mainly on small rodents and birds, but since I wanted Penny to grow strong bones and teeth, I determined to go on feeding her.

There were some termite hills on the limestone plain; in the rest of Shaba they were rare, for the lava was too hard for the building require-ments of the ants. Penny loved these hillocks, so we made a point of going by them on our walks. I was intrigued at the way in which she seemed to have a foreknowledge of my intentions; even before I had told Makedde that I wished to go past the ant-hills she had made off in their direction as though she was already aware of my plans.

Even if it is generally accepted that animals can often read our minds, Penny seemed to be especially gifted in anticipating plans of which I myself was still unaware. I do not believe that this arose from what we call intelligence. It probably comes from some sense beyond our perception.

We now made a point of ending our afternoon walk by the lion pool where jackals, gerenuk, Grant's gazelle, and Kori bustard often came for their afternoon drink. When we left her we hid behind some bushes and observed Penny, trembling with excitement as she watched the Grant's gazelle grazing within a few meters of her. When it got dark we went home. Next morning we found no evidence of a kill.

One evening when the light was fading, we saw Penny chasing a cheetah, but we were not able to see how the pursuit ended. This was the first cheetah we had seen in Shaba. After Penny had spent ten days near the lion pool, the gazelles went off, whereupon she returned to the base of Turkana Hill. Here the limestone plain was covered with bushes, now in full flower. The variety in the shape and color of the blooms gave me the impression of Elysian fields.

Penny soon discovered a little hole filled with rainwater, and went there to quench her thirst. It would be impossible to imagine a more enchanting scene than that of the leopardess drinking from a pool surrounded by flower-covered bushes against a background of red, rocky mountains. When the rains stopped and the sun dried up the pool, we refilled it daily. Makedde christened it Penny's Bar.

One morning she met her first giraffe and bolted, terrified. When she reemerged, she was obviously still very frightened, even though I stroked her and encouraged her in a low, reassuring voice. This was the largest animal she had yet seen, and I thought that if I had been in her place, I too would have been frightened.

This incident made me realize how much young wild animals need to be taught by their mothers regarding the danger that other species might be to them. Although they have innate instincts to rely on, as evidenced by the care Penny took to avoid crossing open ground, the fact that she had had no training from her mother was a great loss to her. This was made obvious when she had no fear of the aardwolf but was alarmed at the sight of a buffalo, which would only attack a leopard if it threatened her calf.

CHAPTER SIX

From Pet
to Wild Leopardess

ONE EVENING I floated into a happy, carefree world, listening to a Strauss waltz on the radio, only to be plunged back suddenly into the ferocity of the bush by a terrifying bellow accompanied by a deep lion's roar. Sinister silence followed. I turned off the radio and heard the agonized groans of some panic-stricken animal accompanied by ear-splitting roars. The heart-rending sounds rose to an unbearable crescendo, after which the moans of the terrified animal ebbed away, and all was again silent.

I recognized that what I had heard were the death cries of a buffalo killed by a lion. For the rest of the night I was haunted by this gruesome incident, and questioned why the joy that the music had given me had been completely obliterated by the horror of this agonizing death. Was it true, I wondered, that fear of death is the driving force that insures our survival?

The killing had involved too long a struggle for it to have been the work of adult lions. In the morning we saw a lioness with two half-grown cubs sneaking out of the reeds at our approach. Plainly the youngsters had been responsible for the death of the buffalo who, to judge by the trampled and blood-stained ground, must have put up a tremendous fight.

The battle had taken place within a few hundred meters of the camp, and I wondered whether the victim had been one of our eleven buffalo friends who had become so used to our presence that they were almost tame. For a few weeks they had been absent, but on the previous evening we had seen them grazing near the camp. During the rain, lions as well as buffalo had avoided the soggy ground; it seemed terribly bad luck if both had returned on the same night. Buffalo meat is highly prized by Africans, and, finding the carcass only half eaten, Makedde cut some strips which, as biltong, would last him for many days.

I was sorry that Penny had not witnessed the kill, but now I understand why yesterday she had stayed on a branch of her treee, something she had not done since September (we were now approaching Christmas). She was certainly clever at avoiding lions, but as regards her natural prey she was completely indifferent. Only that evening we had observed her with Grant's gazelles which, as the wind was in our favor, we approached to within 60 meters without their becoming aware of our presence. Penny had not seen them, so we literally turned her around to face them. She was not at all interested, spun around, and then sat down and looked at us.

"Go, Penny, go!" I whispered. Since this had no effect I pushed her gently toward them; observing this, the gazelles snorted and advanced toward us. Penny immediately placed herself between Makedde and me. I gave her another push which produced no result, after which we all went forward using cover afforded by the bushes. Penny accompanied us but kept looking at me as though asking what she was supposed to do. The situation was ridiculous. I went ahead, the gazelles ran some 40 meters and then stopped in a line facing us. Again I whispered, "Go, go!" to Penny, and this time she responded, taking careful cover as she moved on alone toward the grazing herd. At this point it became dark and we had to go home, so we did not see the outcome of my maneuvering of Penny.

During the night I wondered what I could do to teach Penny to hunt. I thought that from the intonation of my voice, not to mention any gift she had for reading my thoughts, she should know what I wanted her to do. Certainly the gazelles had sized Penny up and did not regard her as a danger, since they went on grazing quite close to her. Was Penny, I questioned, at 15 months, still too young to tackle such large antelopes, or even their fawns? Her reactions convinced me that the gazelle killed a few weeks ago near the camp was not her victim, though I was convinced it had been killed by a leopard. Yet, except for the spoor that we had once found near Turkana Hill, we had never seen any trace of another leopard.

We were now having some difficulty in locating Penny if she was more than 50 meters away, because of some fault in the radio collar. Luckily it was nearly Christmas and we were expecting George for the holidays. Since he had used radio collars on many of his lions, we knew he would be able to help mend ours.

He and Patrick Hamilton arrived early on the evening of Christmas Eve. We went off to find Penny, who was near the place where we had left her that morning. She showed no fear of George or Patrick, and followed us back to the car in which we had left the tools needed to repair her radio collar. Then she crept under a nearby bush. I kept my eye on her in case she might be tempted to jump at the men while they were sitting on the ground surrounded by screws, nuts, and bolts. However, they were left in peace and the vital part of the receiver was adjusted.

Penny meanwhile retired to such a dense part of the bush that we could not see her. I was unable to resist taking a photograph of George, Patrick, and the two assistants crawling on their hands and knees into the thicket while Penny made off from the opposite side. After this Patrick had to fly back to Meru while we went home to our Christmas dinner.

I had dressed a little Christmas tree, using a seedling balanites tree from whose many thorns I hung my decorations. These I had improvised by cutting stars and glitter from foil wrappings of chocolate and medicine. For candlesticks I used the tops of fruit juice bottles which I filled with sand. I grouped them around the tree and the presents. It was a happy evening. For the next few days Penny remained near Turkana Hill, and we spent our time walking with her or fishing.

For George the place had nostalgic memories of the time when, twenty years ago, he had been in charge of the area. Then he had been surrounded by great herds of Grevy's and Burchell's zebra and many elephants and antelopes, not to mention smaller game. We had now spent three months in Shaba and had not seen a single elephant, though we had found a bleached skeleton which gave testimony of the extent of the poaching taking place. I collected a shoulder blade and pelvis bones and grouped them around the camp fence. This, I thought, would express our challenge to reverse the years of destruction. Already I was gratified to see that many Grant's gazelles, gerenuk, and herds of the usually elusive oryx antelope today grazed peacefully within a few meters of us, whereas in September they had bolted at the sound of our car.

There were at this time very few tourists in Shaba, and we were the
only people living there. Soon the animals realized that we meant them
no harm, and later they accepted us as friends. The local fauna included
two prides of lion who, after staying close to the camp for several days,
watched us passing by in our car without being in any way disturbed.

Fishing along the river was idyllic. Its banks were shaded by doum
palms, fig trees, and poplars. It is true that we had to keep a look out
for crocodiles, and, in the thick bush, for buffaloes; but, listening to the
water bubbling over the shoals, the wind rustling through the palms, the
rhythm of their swinging fronds and the haunting cry of a pair of
crested cranes, I felt that we had gone back in time, back to the days
when George and I spent months on safari in the Northern Frontier District where man was quite unimportant. Today George's hair was white,
but as we picnicked by the river and I watched him patiently throwing
his line again and again until he got a bite, it was as though time had
been telescoped.

A little farther down the stream Kifosha was fishing, and still farther
away Makedde was trying his luck. All four of us enjoyed the beautiful
surroundings, perhaps even more than the landing of a barbel or a
catfish.

Before George left on the twenty-eighth, he went to say good-bye to
Penny. We found her very excited. As usual she hated being photographed, and when George took a shot she made a flying leap at me and
tore a gash across my collarbone. It was not deep, but even after treating
it with Tetracycline ointment, it took weeks to heal.

During the holidays Martin developed malaria and had to go for two
weeks to Nanyuki hospital; then, soon after his return, he fell against
the sharp edge of a table and got such a bad concussion that we were
obliged to call the flying doctor who took him to Nairobi hospital.

Deprived of her playmate, Penny's games of hide-and-seek and ambushing were reduced—she was too strong for me, and I kept Makedde
as a buffer between her and myself whenever she was in a jumping
mood. She was quick to develop new tactics and decided to ambush us
only when we had the sun directly in our eyes and were blinded by it.
Naturally we tried to move to another position, but she usually was
cunning enough to outwit us, and in the end the changing of positions
came to be the point of the game rather than the ambushing itself.

Another of her sports was to enter some hyena burrows now occupied
by bats. Here she had great fun waking them from their daytime sleep

and wriggling forward to block their escape route. Her interest in these creatures made me wonder if bats feature on a leopard's menu.

A week later Penny left Turkana Hill and moved 4 kilometers to a lava flow adjoining the limestone plain. She skipped light-footedly across the boulders concealed by high grass, but for me the walking was very difficult.

After the rains there were many birds' nests hidden among the rocks. One day Penny stepped on two sandgrouse chicks whose coloring provided a perfect camouflage. One died, whereupon she carried the body to a bush and left it there. Since she made no attempt to eat it, I hand-fed it to her.

During the night we heard lions' roars coming from the direction of Turkana Hill. This made me realize why Penny had abandoned it. After five days the lions left, and she returned.

One morning I took off my canvas gloves while feeding her, and put them on a nearby bush. I could take this risk because, during her feeding sessions, Penny was always very gentle and took care not to hurt my fingers, but now, when she spotted the gloves, she seized them and dashed off with them. When I tried to get them away from her she bit a large hole in my left arm. Because I had much more contact with Penny than had Martin I was far more vulnerable than he, but since I had survived many painful scratches from Elsa and Pippa, I took her bites in my stride.

As she had an advantage over me on uneven ground, we tried to lead her to the base of Turkana Hill by withholding water from her. This worked well for a few days, during which she was particularly affectionate.

One evening Penny was awakened by an oryx who, unaware of our presence, passed within some 50 meters of us. Instantly she started stalking the antelope. Wriggling close to the ground and keeping under cover, she advanced slowly, but when the oryx looked up she froze. This went on for about ten minutes, by which time Penny was close enough to charge; but at that moment the oryx got her scent and rushed off, she followed it, and eventually we lost sight of the pair. I could not think why Penny was unafraid of so big a beast, weighing some 180 kilograms, and whose rapier-like horns caused it to be given a wide berth by most animals. It must, I thought, be the valor of ignorance.

Now, again, we observed a slight secretion coming from her vulva; if she were once more in oestrus this could explain both her present need for affection and also her tendency to jump at us. On January 14 she moved halfway toward the Ridge. We found her in a densely wooded lugga which, judging by the many spoor, was a lay-up for buffaloes. To reach it we had to stagger across an area of uneven lava overgrown by prickly grass whose spines penetrated our trousers.

Even though the radio signals indicated that we were close to Penny, we had to call for a quarter of an hour before she emerged from an almost impenetrable thicket. She was very thirsty, but even when drinking, she looked back continually into the thicket and was plainly listening intently. She refused to eat the meat we had brought, and soon disappeared. However, when we returned in the afternoon she was hungry as well as thirsty. I presumed that there might be a male around.

Next day we received no radio signal even though we climbed every hill in the area in the hope of getting a reading. It was very annoying not to be able to trace Penny just when we thought she might be with a mate, and when she had moved farther from camp than she had till now; besides, I was haunted by the thought that she might have been taken by a crocodile when she was drinking in the river.

About this time a bush fire caused me considerable anxiety. It was several kilometers wide and was approaching the camp. Although it was still a long way off, a blanket of black smoke hung over the mountains and the plain. Everyone was busy cutting a firebreak, but we had little hope of stopping the flames unless the high wind dropped. Fortunately at about nine in the evening this happened.

Not much later, a group of Africans appeared, shouting and brandishing their spears. Their appearance along the camp fence was rather frightening, but it turned out that they were only Meru tribesmen in search of some cattle of theirs which had been stolen. We gave them hospitality till dawn, when they moved off.

The wind having dropped completely, and the smoldering fire being far away, we resumed our search for Penny. Starting from the lugga where we had last seen her and avoiding the black cotton plains which were waterlogged, we reached the granite Ridge which formed a picturesque outline and contrasted with the densely wooded country below. As we walked up the slope we saw many gerenuk and Grant's gazelles on the lower levels, and higher up, hares and birds. This was ideal leopard country. From the top of the Ridge we were able to see that it ran parallel with the river and was intersected by several ravines which went down to the water.

Suddenly we received weak signals from the direction of the river. We realized that the ravines made splendid leopard lanes since they provided hideouts between their steep walls and tumbled boulders, and were shaded by dense vegetation. I had always feared that Penny might make her way to the river which formed the northern boundary of Shaba. Once there, having had no mother to warn her against crocodiles, she would be very vulnerable. Also she could easily cross at some shallow point and make her way into the strictly prohibited military zone where there were high mountains and rocky cliffs among which we could not follow her should she decide to make her home there.

Waving the antenna, we struggled through bush and outcrops till we found a rough cart track wending its way to the river. Here we nearly stumbled over Penny crouching under a bush. A lion or a cheetah would have given some sound when it saw us, but Penny remained silent, and as her spotted fur blended perfectly with the sun-flecked ground, it was no wonder that she was so difficult to locate. After two days on her own, she was pleased to see us and rubbed herself against our legs.

I observed that her belly was full. Of course I was relieved to see her fit and well and still within Shaba territory, but I wanted to get her away from the vicinity of the river.

When on our return journey we reached the top of the Ridge, we saw that the bush fire had flared up again, so we hurried back to the camp. A team sent by Hussein, the Assistant Warden, was cutting a firebreak, and as our help was not needed we returned to look for Penny. We found her where we had left her and it took a lot of coaxing to induce her to come to the top of the Ridge. There we left her food and water, and went home hoping that tomorrow she would still be at the same spot.

Next day, when we met Penny, she was already on her way to the river. Since the morning was cool and the sky overcast, she was more energetic than she had been recently, and consented to follow us to the top of the Ridge, down the slope facing Turkana Hill, and right out onto the plain below. While we were feeding her there was a sudden icy blast of wind followed by a cloudburst. We huddled together for protection, for the whipping rain was so violent that it actually hurt our skins. Poor Penny, standing in the open, numb with cold, looked terrified. The ground was already ankle deep in water. In all the forty years I had lived in Kenya, I had never experienced such a storm, and since it showed no sign of letting up, we decided to go home, slithering and splashing along, frozen to the bone.

I kept close to Penny, patting her at intervals in an effort to reassure her. After a while she suddenly raced back to the Ridge and reached safe ground, but for us there were four wet, cold hours ahead as we plodded to camp.

This sudden change from great heat to great cold was frightening, but at least the torrential rain had extinguished the bush fire. Uncomfortable as it had been, we were in fact lucky, for later over the radio we heard about some very disastrous effects of the storm.

The ground next morning was still too wet to drive to the Ridge, so we had a long, tiring walk before we found Penny. Again, she was near the river, and as it was by then eleven o'clock, it was very hot and if we meant to cajole her back to Turkana Hill we must start at once.

Relying on Penny's fondness for ambushing, we hid behind bush after bush, and so lured her on till she stopped, panting, in the shade of a tree from which nothing would move her. I sat beside her, her head in my lap, stroking her till she dozed off. When she woke we went on, taking frequent rests. I was touched to see how Penny dragged herself along and then waited for me to return to her and stroke her. We had not expected to make a whole day's expedition, and had therefore not brought any water for ourselves and so by now we were both thirsty and exhausted. Suddenly Makedde remembered a little water-table in the rocks which he thought might be full after the storm. We made our way to it. I drank, cupping my hands. Penny and Makedde lapped. I mention this because it is generally believed that only Australian Aborigines lap, whereas I have often seen Africans in remote parts of the country drinking in this way. This drink seemed to me better than any water we had tasted, and gave us the necessary impetus to carry on.

Advancing slowly, we reached a narrow lugga with wooded banks, close to Turkana Hill. By now it was getting dark, and here Penny stayed put.

When I reached camp I found that Martin had returned from Nairobi hospital and that for the last hour he and Jock had been watching our activities through field-glasses. They had brought fruit juice for Makedde and myself and meat for Penny—a good addition to our stores.

On the following day we got a reading which told us that Penny was back on the Ridge. She looked superb as she emerged from a crevice high up on a cliff. She quickly responded to my call, but stopped at some distance from us and waited for me to bring her meat and water. As soon as she had finished her meal she raced back to the crevice and vanished.

Again I wondered whether at last she might have found a mate, for her behavior had changed surprisingly. Yesterday she had been affectionate, whereas today she not only refused to join us for a walk but did not allow me to touch her. Twenty-four hours later she was her normal self again, delighted to see Martin after his month's absence. We walked along the well-worn path leading to the crest of the Ridge, which Makedde told us was known locally as Rhino Ridge because in the distant past there had been many rhinos there. Later, before Shaba became a Reserve, they had been killed off by poachers who used this path when hunting. Nearby was an overgrown cart track leading up to the hills. Searching for pug marks of any animals that had been around during the night we learned that a jackal, two hyenas, and two lions had followed the track.

After gamboling along for two hours, Penny led us back to the area where she had spent the last two days. Here she leaped onto a shady ledge on an overhanging cliff from which she could watch the luggas nearby as well as the plains below. We relaxed together. I stroked her silky coat and was happy that I had achieved such a good rapport with her; she seemed to love and trust me. This was a different kind of relationship than the ones I had had with my previous wild animals; my rapport with Elsa, for example, had seemed to be an intuitive one, whereas the bond with Penny was one of intelligence. Her mind was never vacant.

Although we had once heard lions in the area, we found Penny in the same place next day. Since she seemed to have the intention of making her home here, we decided to hide a 4-gallon can of water in a cleft. This would enable us to place a basin nearby, well hidden under a bush, which we could fill from a can; in this way Penny would still have water when the rock pool dried up. In Swahili a basin is called a *karai*, so now we christened this area Karai Rocks.

During our next drive to Penny we came upon a black-maned lion near the track. He was moving away from the Ridge. We found Penny standing in the open as though waiting for us; she was in a jumping mood but when I said "No!" she would stop in midair, and after landing, lie on her back looking at me and nibbling her hind legs. She was very excitable and waited till I was far enough from Makedde to enable her to jump straight at me, scratching my arm quite deeply through my canvas gloves.

While Martin and I fed her, Makedde searched for her lair and found it under a cliff by an almost impenetrable thicket next to an abandoned porcupine burrow. Strategically it was an admirable site.

It was now the end of January 1978, and for the last three days Penny had appeared to be in oestrus. The symptoms we observed were:

1. Her exceptionally silky fur.
2. A slight discharge from her vulva.
3. Loss of appetite.
4. An increased demand for affection.

For the first time in Shaba I saw Penny marking her territory by jetting her glandular secretion onto bushes along the path. I took this as an indication that she was intending to make the Ridge her permanent home. I could not imagine a more perfect location, and was delighted when Makedde told me it was not long since the area had been visited by leopards.

Penny was now 18 months old, the age at which in normal circumstances she would become independent of her mother; but during our walks I was still following immediately behind her, and I wondered whether her tendency to jump at me might arise from a dislike of my keeping so near to her. I therefore decided to keep near to Makedde and at a good distance from Penny, but the only result was that she tripped him up and growled at him; apparently she did not want her games with me spoiled. Makedde, however, was firm—he either ignored her antics or addressed her in an authoritative voice, "No, Penny, *no!*" Certainly she respected him and, indeed, he seemed to have more control over her than did the rest of us.

One morning, when Penny was exceptionally busy jetting bushes along our path, we observed her stalking a porcupine. She jumped around it from all angles, trying to get at its head while keeping at a safe distance. In the end the porcupine raised its quills and scuttled away. I was glad to see Penny treating this living pin-cushion with caution; although the quills are not poisonous, if they break off and become embedded in the flesh, the area becomes infected and painful. That same morning we saw some fresh leopard spoors.

Penny, having been born at an altitude of 2,000 meters, needed far more water than local leopards who were adjusted from birth to the heat of Shaba. Since by now all the puddles had dried up, Karai was Penny's only drinking place unless she were to go to the river, from which we were anxious to keep her away. We were therefore concerned that Karai should keep clear, so we placed a small stone in it which acted as a ladder for small lizards and beetles who kept the water clean.

From now on Penny continued to mark her territory, which again made me wonder whether she were pregnant. Certainly we had seen leopard spoor when she was last in oestrus. We watched her nipples with growing interest, even though I knew that in lions and cheetahs signs of pregnancy become obvious only at a late date. Finally I could no longer contain my curiosity and sent a sample of urine to the veterinary laboratory. But the reply came that the test for human pregnancy did not work for animals, so all we could do was wait, and while doing so, feed Penny well. I began to dip her pieces of meat into bone meal, taking care that no dry powder remained on the pieces because if it did she would not swallow a morsel.

One day, after a two-hour walk with Penny, we settled down for a picnic lunch, intending to spend the day with her. Martin took out a book, and I my painting gear, but no sooner did Penny see my sketchbook than she woke up and made a grab at it. I got it back with difficulty, after which she went off to doze under a nearby bush. Makedde had left, carrying his rifle along, when suddenly a bedlam of baboon shrieks shattered the silence. I rushed over to where Penny had been sleeping, but found she had gone. This did not surprise me as wherever I looked I saw baboons jumping off rocks and trees, barking loudly. I was anxious because if the baboons attacked Penny she would not stand a chance; their canines are much larger than those of a leopard and they would tear her to pieces in a few minutes.

Martin grabbed the radio antenna, and we followed its weak signals, while the baboons, alarmed by our presence, moved off. Eventually we located Penny under a bush; she was panting, no doubt because she had run 4 kilometers during the hot hours of the day. She seemed pleased to see us, and rubbed herself against our legs. As the bush she was lying under was small, and provided only enough shade for her, we induced her to follow us to the top of the Ridge where we could all relax in the shade of a tree.

Penny had dragged herself along, obviously very tired, but suddenly she became alert to the slightest rustle of a leaf or flight of a bird, to anything in fact that could be a signal of approaching danger. Only now did I realize how much she had changed from a confident pet to a wild leopardess, always listening and prepared to confront a threat, while remaining loving and in need of a lot of affection. Whenever we stroked or patted her she responded by sometimes jumping at us or patting us, but the moment we scolded her she stopped and obviously tried her best to remain quiet, though there always came a moment when this was too much for her, and she jumped at us again.

When the heat grew less, we walked back to the Karai and here we left Penny. After the day's events I was glad to know that her fear of baboons was such that it would make her bolt for a long distance even during the heat of the day.

Next day we sighted her licking a paw in an unsuccessful endeavor to extract a thorn embedded between her toes. Patiently she let me pull it out even though this must have been quite a painful operation. While engaged in this I observed that she had a maggot embedded in one of her hind legs, and that the area around it had gone septic, probably because she had tried to remove it before it was ready to drop off. Again she cooperated while I squeezed the maggot out; then she licked the wound clean. After all this, to cheer her up, we gave her some marrow— a special treat, for, like Elsa and Pippa, she greatly preferred marrow to meat, zebra marrow being the greatest treat of all.

Makedde now went off for a week's leave. During his absence Jock carried the rifle. Penny was suspicious of him, and would only follow Martin and me if he were out of sight.

Recently we had noticed a crack in Penny's radio collar, and I had brought some fast-drying glue with which to mend it at the first opportunity. So the next time she lay sleepily under a shady rock, Martin and I set to work to mend the collar. Then Jock appeared, and immediately Penny gave a leap and bolted. We suggested to Jock that he should leave us and go somewhere where Penny could not see him. Once he was out of sight she came back, and I began to feed her. We always carried her meat in a small canvas basket, and her water in an aluminum milk can. Suddenly she grabbed the basket, which was close by, and rushed off with it. Martin and I ran after her, but it took a lot of time and cunning to recover it. When we had done so I asked Martin to take it to Jock, out of Penny's reach. While he was gone Penny was very gentle and I took off my canvas glove to stroke her; suddenly she turned and, quick as lightning, tore a hole in my arm. I nearly fainted with the pain; this was much the worst bite she had given me, and it required attention, so we drove 30 kilometers to the Mission hospital, where five stitches were put in to close the wound.

It was lucky that the incident took place the night before the rains broke and the roads turned to mud. In spite of these conditions, the next morning we succeeded in driving close to Penny's Ridge and located her in a rocky lugga. When Jock came near she became very nervous; there was no doubt that his presence upset her, so I asked him to drive to Isiolo and bring Makedde back.

Soon after he had gone some weekend guests arrived, unheralded because their attempts to contact us by letter and radio had been unsuccessful. We had hardly settled them in before a downpour turned the camp into a quagmire. Heavy rain drummed on the roof; my arm had swollen a lot; and by 9:00 P.M. we decided to go to bed. A little later Jock arrived soaked to the skin because the car had broken down on Turkana Hill and he had had to walk from there. We spent our time next day winching out the Toyota. Fortunately the rain stopped, so at ten Jock set off to pick up Makedde.

My friends were leaving next day, and as my arm was very swollen and turning black, we arranged to drive in convoy to Nanyuki where I could consult another doctor. He removed the stitches of catgut, which had infected the wound, and insisted that I should stay a few days under his care.

When I returned to Shaba it had been eight days since I had seen Penny. She was delighted at my arrival, and never left my side. I learned that she had spent the time of my absence in her new lair. One excitement had been her encounter with a genet which was hiding in a thicket. Penny had hissed at it, besieged it, and it had hissed back at her, after which it had run away and disappeared into a hole. Martin inspected the cavity, and found it was the entrance to a porcupine's burrow. It had two more entrances some 10 meters apart, and this suggested that it might even be large enough to accommodate a leopard. We were glad to know this in case Penny should decide to hide there. It was also the sort of place that Penny might choose for giving birth to her cubs.

For the moment, however, the only interest it held for her was connected with the genet. She stayed inside one of the entrance tunnels while Martin guarded the other two. Later Martin went home, leaving Penny to her vigil. From this time onwards, the lugga became known as Genet Lugga.

Now that I was back, we cajoled Penny to Karai, where we fed her and stayed nearby until she became sleepy. Makedde complained that he had had a bad toothache during my absence, but did not wish to leave camp to go to a dentist until I had returned. Now he wanted to go to the hospital at Isiolo and have the tooth taken out, so he and Jock drove off, leaving Martin and me to cope with Penny.

When we met again, Penny seemed to be as happy as I was. We spent all morning coaxing her back to Karai. To reassure her, we returned at midday, parking the car in the usual place close to the junction of two tracks leading down to the river. Up to now we had done our best to keep Penny away from these tracks, because they were visited by tourists; also, there were some great rocks nearby which were favored by baboons. Indeed, we had seen them settling down for the night on small ledges on the vertical face of the cliff, shelves that were hardly visible and certainly out of reach of a leopard or other predator.

I was therefore far from pleased to see Penny halfway up the rock gazing hard at a herd of Grant's gazelles on the plain below. This was the last area I wished her to frequent, but she seemed fascinated by the view, and for a long time ignored my calls. Eventually she came down, drank, and followed us slowly back to Karai where she settled between the two of us and was soon asleep.

There was no sound except for the wind and Penny's breathing, and no movement except for that of a spider killing a beetle ten times its size which had got caught in the net, probably intended for some butterflies dancing nearby, quite unaware of any danger. In the great heat, life seemed to stand still.

I was touched that although we had abandoned her early in the morning and enticed her to take a walk at the hottest time of the day, so far as Penny was concerned it seemed that we could do no wrong. This worried me because we were at present her only friends and, as such, might become too deeply imprinted upon her.

Since we did not think she had encountered a mate as yet, let alone become pregnant, we decided to build a boma for the leopard we intended to import for her.

CHAPTER SEVEN

Kula, the Lion Cub

IT WAS NOT easy to find a suitable place in which to build a home for Penny's future mate. It had to be accessible by car, but it must be concealed from tracks that were in use, and it must be somewhere where there was no danger of its becoming waterlogged during the rains. Finally, it must have bushes around it to provide shade and concealment in the weeks during which the leopard would be recovering from the shock of being trapped and transported to Shaba. Eventually we decided on a place at the base of Turkana Hill, 4 kilometers from Penny's Ridge, and facing it. The holding home was to be 13 meters long by 8 meters wide and divided by wire mesh into two equal sections. Three doors would make it possible to close the section occupied by the leopard so that we could safely place meat and water in the other section. Once this had been done, we could open the door and let the leopard in to have his meal. Half the boma would be covered by a roof made of reeds which would provide shade; this section would contain the few bushes that were growing in the area. There would also be a wooden platform to which the leopard could retire if, for instance, the ground was invaded by safari ants. The walls and all the roofing would be covered with wire mesh secured to posts 3 meters high.

Under normal circumstances the boma could be completed in two weeks, but with the onset of the rains and the fact that only casual labor was available, it might well take six weeks to complete the job.

It was now that Penny surprised us by giving the famous leopard grunts while playing with us. So far she had only occasionally growled when defending a tennis ball or meat at Elsamere.

The rains were so heavy that it was impossible for us to drive to Penny's Ridge so we had a long walk to reach it. She always was delighted to see us and ambushed us vigorously; however, unlike Elsa's cubs who always attacked from the rear, Penny came straight at us.

When we got back to camp we found a tiny lion cub, all ears and eyes, crouching in the farthest corner of the wired-in enclosure. It looked terrified.

I was so excited when I saw the cub that at first I did not notice that there was a note for me. It was from the Warden, and read as follows:

Dear Joy:
I have been at your camp for the last 3½ hours and you did not turn up. I passed your Toyota parked on the way and thought you would come back early. The purpose of my visit was to bring you this lion cub found abandoned by its mother in the Samburu Reserve. My ranger brought it on Thursday night and I have taken care of it in my house, feeding it with milk. I had to transfer the cub to you because of the tourists coming to the house to see and photo it. This made my house like a zoo or museum with mini-buses parked everywhere. I intend to rear this little cub until such time when it can be returned to the wild. I am not giving it to anybody for I shall be keeping it around my house. Please take care of it for the time being, then later I shall take it away. I'll be seeing you shortly on this issue. Yours,

Bob Oguya, Warden
12 March 1978

My first task was to feed the cub, which had had nothing to eat for some time. I mixed a teaspoonful of glucose and two drops of Abidec into one part of Nestlé's milk and one part water. As I had no nipples for a feeding bottle, I was obliged to use a syringe. After a struggle I managed to get a cupful of the mixture down the cub's throat. Then I placed a cardboard box and a wooden box with a wire door inside the enclosure. The cub would not enter either but hid behind them. Next I tried to make friends with him, holding out my hand so that he could get my scent. The result was a sharp nip from well-developed teeth; by this I judged that he must be 6 or 7 weeks old. He was very thin, with his pelvis bones sticking out. I also saw that he had several large, cherry-red swellings, surely due to maggots.

Knowing that no baby animal likes being left alone, I arranged for grass to be laid on the floor of the wooden box and for a cloth to be hung over it. After this the hutch was placed next to my bed so that I would be able to reassure the cub during the night.

Neither of us got much sleep, for the cub only dozed for brief spells when he had completely exhausted himself crying. During the night he made more different sounds than any lion cub I had known. They ranged from high-pitched chirps to a deep little roar, all expressing distress. To add to the cub's unhappiness, some lions must have been close to the camp, for we heard their growls; perhaps they had been attracted by the cub's pitiful cries.

When dawn broke I carried the cub into Penny's large enclosure. Discovering it contained a bush, he went at once to hide behind it. I was glad that the boma was large enough for the cub to get a certain amount of exercise, since this was vital for his digestion to function naturally, and I did not want him to become dependent on laxatives. Knowing that if he were with his mother she would lick the anus to stimulate the defecation of feces, I wiped the area with a damp cloth. While doing so I tried to sex it, and discovered that it was a male.

I named the little lion Kula, short for *chakula*, which means food in Swahili. He needed to eat every two and a half hours. Knowing from experience that lion cubs begin to eat meat when they are only 5 weeks old, I now added a handful of mincemeat, a teaspoonful of Farex, a teaspoonful of bone meal, a tablet of calcium, and a little salt to his Abidec, and mixed the lot into milk. Kula could not get enough of this brew, and after finishing it was so contented that he even allowed me to wipe his mouth with a damp cloth to keep the hair around his lips clean.

As I was sure that he should not be left alone, I had to give up my daily searches for Penny and leave that task to Martin and Makedde. On the first day they did the best they could, but after an eight-hour walk they returned defeated. While they were away I had been busily inventing games for Kula. I wrapped a tennis ball in newspaper, attached it to a string, and swung the contraption around him. He very soon got the idea, and chased after it, showing remarkably quick reactions.

When he was tired and resting, I was able to squeeze six maggots out of his skin. They are very common among wild animals, for they drop their eggs onto moist ground so that if later a beast rolls in it, the eggs get attached to its skin. These develop into maggots which cause swellings that eventually burst, and so the cycle is repeated. Kula's coat was very badly affected by them. I could only hope that by feeding him well five times a day (but never during the night) his condition would improve.

Like all wild animals he hated being obliged to foul his sleeping place, but since he could not get out of his box during the night, this was inevitable. Inevitable, too, that my tent was thereby flooded. However, for the moment this was something we both had to put up with. The cub quickly learned that when I called, "Kula, Kula, Kulala!" I was about to offer him some delicious food, so of course he emerged at once from wherever he was hiding and made for his feeding bowl. While he was busy eating I was able to remove ticks and burrs from his coat.

Kula's spots were exceptionally dark for a lion born in this arid area. The large square or oblong patches (they are not really spots, though this is what they are called) ran into each other like the markings of a reticulated giraffe and, like Penny, Kula had a line of parallel dark patches running from the root of his tail along his spine. The leopardess also had an exceptionally long line of ten parallel rosettes; Kula had only four such markings. I was much intrigued at being able to compare the overlapping designs of such markings in a lion and a leopard. To record them I both photographed and sketched them from every angle. I had plenty of time to do this and I spent all day with the frightened cub trying to reassure him. He seemed to like my massaging his hard little tummy as he lay on his back pedaling with his four legs. At night, when he was boxed, I imitated his various calls as best I could in an effort to comfort him. All the same, neither of us got much sleep. There was no doubt that his quarters were too small, so I sent a message to Jock in Nanyuki asking him to have a much bigger box made.

Since I was expecting the Warden to come to see him, I asked Makedde and Martin to search for Penny while I stayed in camp; their search was unsuccessful. In the evening there was a heavy rainstorm which frightened Kula so much that I thought I had better keep him in my study tent while I was typing letters. Unfortunately he found so many things to investigate and then tear to pieces that it was not long before I was obliged to take him back to his box. The arrival of the larger box improved matters, but again in the morning I found my tent flooded.

Feeling that I could not neglect Penny for too long, I arranged that Kifosha should feed Kula in the mornings while I went off to find the leopardess.

On my first expedition it took from 7:00 A.M. to 4:00 P.M. to locate her, so when I got back, very tired, I found an extremely lonely cub who gave me a most affectionate welcome: licking my face, hanging on to me, and wanting to play till it was dark. There was no doubt that Kula was extremely intelligent and had a fine personality.

Gratefully I reflected that I had a unique and fascinating life: here I was, spending most of the day searching for a wild leopardess who was probably sharing her life with a mate but who, when she heard my voice, came bounding out of her hiding place to rub herself against my legs; and when I returned to camp, it was to find an affectionate baby lion waiting for me, for whom I represented mother, food, security, and play. On the other hand, I was relieved to know that not only was Penny truly wild, but that Kula's instincts were unimpaired. The latter was proved by the fact that he always covered his feces with earth or leaves, like a grown-up lion, and also that he had succeeded in catching and killing a fledgling pigeon.

I soon realized that Kula had teething problems, for he chewed on any hard object he could find. I therefore gave him a meaty bone; discovering that this new toy was edible, he tore the meat to shreds. Another discovery of his was that it was fun to climb. One day I found him stretched out on one of Penny's platforms from which he could view all that went on in the camp. He must have reached it by clambering up the log ladder we had made for the leopardess. Kula practiced climbing daily, sticking his sharp little claws into the back of the logs and then slowly heaving his fat tummy up while I stayed nearby in case he got stuck.

It did not take him long to realize that he was in no danger from anyone in the camp, but he became much alarmed when he heard some vervet monkeys calling to each other. They were some distance away, but he roared as loudly as he could in their direction. Until the Warden turned up it was impossible to plan Kula's future, and I was worried in case I might become permanently imprinted on him. Also, I could not see how the Warden was going to be able to rear him near his house, which was only a few meters away from the staff quarters of the Samburu Lodge. In my anxiety I thought of George, hoping that he might be able to rehabilitate Kula with his fifteen lions and I radio-called him, but he could not take the cub because at the moment Kora was positively saturated with predators. My next thought was of a large privately owned Game Sanctuary not far from our camp, but when I inquired I found that the proprietor did not include predators among his guests. I could not keep Kula for much longer as it was plainly impossible for me to be simultaneously a foster-mother to a leopardess and a lion; each was a full time job and, worse still, lions and leopards are natural enemies.

As the days passed I became increasingly afraid that Kula was destined to lifelong captivity in a zoo. At 8 weeks he was at an age when he would either become fatally imprinted on human beings and never grow to be truly wild, or if fate were very kind and we were able to find his mother, there was a chance—a small chance—that he might be accepted by his pride.

Meanwhile, his need to wet his bed by night drove him frantic, so I put a small mountain tent made of nylon inside the boma next to his sleeping box and I left the door that faced my bed open so that he would know that I was close by. However, I had not allowed for his curiosity. He spent that night tearing the tent, chewing my foam-rubber mattress, crawling over me, and nibbling my toes. Thus occupied, he was very happy but I was not, and finally I had to lock him up again in his box, after which his roars of protest kept the whole camp awake.

My next attempt to give him a place in which to relieve himself during the night was to place Penny's large traveling crate inside the boma and close to the wire. When bedtime came I coaxed Kula into the crate which by now had been covered with grass and then I sat at the door till he felt sleepy. Unfortunately when he woke up and found himself alone he complained loudly, so I had to get up and assure him that I was not far away but when I returned to bed he again uttered loud protests. Thus it continued on succeeding nights till, hardening my heart, I decided that I must stay in bed and remain deaf to his yells; when at last a night passed with only an occasional protest I felt that this was a real achievement.

Kula was a very energetic little lion and needed more exercise than he could get pacing along the wire fence of the boma, so one afternoon I carried him outside the camp into knee-high swamp grass. Instantly he dashed into a small thicket for cover, but soon followed me along the ridges we had made in the soft grass. On either side the grass was so tall that he could not look over the top of it, and this seemed to make him feel secure so long as I was close to him; but when it came to crossing open ground he panicked and rushed back to his grassy cover.

Kula was always on the lookout for danger; if crested cranes or swarms of quelea flew over us he crouched low with flattened ears and froze. If, on the other hand, he decided to bolt, he ran so fast that I could not keep up with him, so I took Makedde to block his escape route.

Kula was very suspicious of Makedde, and only moved when he was safely behind us and I was close in front. This was a healthy reaction, for it seemed to prove that Kula accepted only me as a friend, and that he was not yet a pet.

One day I weighed him, placing him in a basket which I attached to a scale—he weighed 7 kilograms. In another month he would be too heavy for me to carry. Then how would I control him outside the camp unless I trained him to walk on a leash? He had now been with me for fifteen days; his coat had a healthy sheen, his appetite was splendid, his digestion was normal though I had occasionally to help with liquid paraffin, and he was quite fit and fat. When the Warden came to see what had happened to the cub he was surprised by how much Kula had grown and delighted to find him in such excellent condition.

Oguya told me Kula's history: he had been one of three cubs in his pride. The Warden saw him on his own and had tried to find the pride but had been unsuccessful until yesterday when a mother with two cubs had appeared not far from the Lodge in the company of another lioness and a lion.

This might solve Kula's problem, so we planned to put out a bait for the pride and, once they had settled down to their meal, to bring the little lion along and hope the lioness was his mother and that she would accept him. We had to act quickly for the lions might move off again, and if Kula stayed longer in the camp he would become irretrievably imprinted on human beings and there would be no alternative but to send him to a zoo. However, trying to get him accepted by the pride involved a certain risk, because by now he had been separated from them for eighteen days. We therefore arranged that I should stand by for the next day or two, ready to accompany Kula to the meeting.

After the Warden had left, a cloudburst flooded the camp. Kula was very frightened, and while I was reassuring him he gave me three sharp nips to remind me that he still had enough of a wild lion in him to play in their fashion, in which biting and tearing at each other's skins was fair game; but when he was gentle and I took him in my arms he would snuggle around my neck, lick my face with his rough tongue, and obviously trust me. Was it, I wondered, already too late to risk his rehabilitation?

Next day I remained in camp so as to be ready to drive Kula to his family and freedom should the Warden contact me. My feelings were a mixture of hope that the cub would be able to return to his natural life, and sadness at losing him. Meanwhile I sketched him during what might well be our last hours together.

The Warden did not come that day, but at three on the following afternoon he arrived and told me that he had left the pride gorging on a kill, and that if we hurried we might still find them close to it.

We then made our plans: the Warden would maneuver his Land-Rover between the lions and my Toyota; we would then lift the crate with Kula inside it to the ground and open its door. The Warden would drive a little way off and we would watch the lions' reactions. Should they attack Kula he would shoot in the air to frighten them away and we would recover the cub.

We loaded Kula in his crate into my car and I sat close to it while Martin drove and Makedde sat beside him. In the Warden's car which accompanied ours were a number of Rangers who would help in the release.

By the time we arrived at the site of the kill it was already 6:00 P.M. The area was covered with dense bush and, owing to the recent heavy rains, the ground was partly under water. Moreover, there were several tourists' cars cruising around looking for the lions, which had disappeared.

The Warden, after placing Rangers on the various tracks to keep the tourists away, asked me to wait with Kula while he tried to locate the pride. Meanwhile a herd of elephants with several small calves appeared and took an exceptionally long time to move off, and then went in the direction in which we assumed the pride to be.

When the Warden returned it was to say he could not find the lions and that as the light was fading I had better take Kula back to Shaba. We must just hope that if tomorrow he could repeat the operation it would be more successful. I was very disappointed.

As by then we were all very thirsty, we went to the Samburu Lodge to get a quick drink before returning to camp, but before the drinks we had ordered had arrived, a Ranger ran in to tell us that the lions were back at the site of the kill. Probably they had been nearby all the time and had simply kept hidden in thick bush while the tourists' cars were around.

We ran back to the cars but when we got to the spot we found another bus at the site, with tourists taking flash photographs of the lions; the Warden asked them to leave, and when they had gone we drove our cars into position.

On one side we saw the mother lioness. Her two cubs were some 30 meters away behind a large bush. The lion was about 100 meters distant in the opposite direction and with him was another lioness. All were watching us.

The Warden drove between the lion and my car, thus shielding us while we lifted Kula in his box to the ground. By then the light had almost gone and the Warden thought we had better postpone the release for another day, so we put the box back in the car. While we were doing this the mother lioness appeared from behind a bush and looked intently at the box; she even ventured a few steps toward the car. Quickly I asked the Rangers to place the box back on the ground, and then opened its door. Having done this we all jumped into the car and drove some 20 meters away. The mother lioness proceeded to walk up to the box, calling all the time in a sort of soft moan. When she was within 15 meters of it Kula walked out and ran to his mother. She gave him a quick sniff and obviously accepted him.

After this she came up to the box, sniffed it thoroughly, then returned to her son, whereupon both walked off to the waiting cubs. The light was just good enough for us to be able to see that Kula was much larger than the other cubs, who now trotted across to their brother and began playing as though they had never been separated. It was now so dark that even using our headlights we were unable to watch them moving out of sight, so we just sat in silence.

I reflected on the uncanny behavior of the mother lioness: even after Kula's box had been lowered from the car the lioness could not have seen or heard or scented him, yet she behaved as though she knew he was there and, undeterred by our presence, acted as only a mother would if she had found her lost child.

I could only explain her sensing Kula's presence by telepathy, of which I had often seen examples in Elsa, Pippa, and their families. Although this sense is today usually beyond our perception, I think that, like most animals who rely on it, we may have been endowed with it before we developed speech or invented writing or mechanical communication, for the few cases of telepathy among human beings which have been proved recently appear to suggest that they are derived from a sense now atrophied in Homo sapiens.

We shone the headlights in the direction of the lion. He had not moved, though the second lioness had disappeared. Then, as we moved off, driving slowly along the winding track, suddenly we came upon the pride—the mother, the three cubs, and the "aunt" lioness. Both lionesses were acting as cushions for the cubs who were crawling and tobogganing over them and pulling at their ears and tails; Kula was plainly bossing the two smaller cubs. I was moved by the relaxed playfulness of this happy family. Our little lion had been separated from his pride for twenty days, the first three of which he had spent among clicking cameras at the Warden's house, and the last seventeen in my camp where he had accepted me as a friend and trusted me. But the moment he recognized his mother he was at once back in his natural life—it was as though the interval had been a dream, or, perhaps, a nightmare.

CHAPTER EIGHT

Blue Tag

THE ARRIVAL OF Kula had prevented me from visiting Penny; during these days we hoped she might have been with a leopard.

On March 15 I found her spoor and got a good signal coming from near the river. I went to that area and called to her till I was hoarse, but she did not show up. At midday, tired and hot, we trudged back to the top of the Ridge, and suddenly almost stumbled over Penny.

She must have heard us calling all through the morning. She was neither thirsty nor hungry, but welcomed a great deal of stroking and patting. Her fur was exceptionally filthy, and when she had yawned off her sleepiness, she walked back to the river. The next day there was again no sign of her although we spent it searching for her in the grilling heat. On the following morning we observed her spoor in the area of the Ridge, which proved that she had been around on the previous day, though she had failed to respond to our calls. At last we located her at the Genet Lugga. She followed us back to Karai where she dozed off. Our next meeting was at Karai, which made me wonder whether this was a sign that her love affair was over.

On March 25 Martin left us for good. Until I could get a replacement for him, Jock offered to help out though, since Penny was still suspicious of him, we agreed that whenever we found her he would return to the car while Makedde and I walked up to her and fed her. This worked well at first, but there came a day when Penny would not join us for a walk, refused food, twice climbed a tree, and kept on hiding from us. But when I moved a short distance away from Makedde she ran up to me and rolled on her back asking to be stroked, after which she settled down and accepted some of the meat I offered her, carried the rest off to the rock, and then vanished. During the next couple of days she behaved in the same way.

All this happened near to the river at a spot where, according to Makedde, leopards had lived not very long ago. This made us hope that she might not be alone.

When we next saw her she was still near the river. Feeding her was a problem, for if I did not wish to be scratched I had to keep close to Makedde, and if I did this she refused to eat.

While we were so shorthanded Penny lost her collar and the transmitting box went wrong as well, so our only hope of locating her was by calling. For two days we got no result, then Makedde went off on a week's leave. Jock and I had therefore to cope with Penny as best we could. Luckily he found the collar lying in a thicket of doum palm seedlings and I was able to slip it around her neck while she was greeting me. He also succeeded in repairing the transmitter, so after this we could again locate Penny by the radar signals.

Being 20 months old, she was ready to mate and to conceive. It was therefore unfortunate that we were unable to import a leopard until the holding boma had been completed. Penny showed her frustration by bundling herself into a ball and nibbling at her hind legs.

One day our radio reading showed that Penny was about 4 kilometers upriver among giant rocky outcrops. To reach her we had to walk over an area covered by patches of salt bush, whose leaves are rich in soda and are used by wild animals instead of a salt lick. We passed some shady acacias and later an unusually saline lake which, owing to the rains, was now quite deep. On this walk I saw a dead snake with a dead lizard sticking out of its mouth. Evidently the snake had found it too large to swallow, the lizard had got stuck and so both had died; this was the first occasion I had come across in which a snake had fatally misjudged the size of its meal.

On the next lap of our trip we passed through a belt of very dense, thorny bush which, judging by the many buffalo pats and old spoor of lions, must have been much used by these beasts as a resting place. Beyond it we entered a real leopard's paradise.

In front of us was a narrow ridge which ran for a kilometer and had walls of sheer cliff on either side; some of its giant boulders had fallen while others remained balanced at a precarious angle. Among these were many crevices and caves which offered Penny a choice of lairs. Near to the cliffs were three outcrops which formed a valley along which we saw car tracks that eventually led to the river.

As we tried to explore the area, we were suddenly confronted by Penny. She must have been watching our approach, and now emerged from behind some rocks. She was very thirsty and kept listening and looking around nervously. As she drank I listened to the sound of her lapping; invariably she lapped in equal numbers before swallowing, and I could judge how thirsty she was by the number of laps which preceded a swallow: the greater the number the greater her thirst. Today was a record for she lapped twelve times in succession.

We concluded that Penny had probably ventured into this new district because she had sensed that there was a male in the vicinity, so as soon as we had fed her we left her.

About 12 kilometers down the track we came upon wide rapids which, when the water was low, would give easy access to the far bank. We named these Rapid Rocks. They caused me some anxiety, for if Penny were to cross here and go over to Bodech mountain range, we should never be able to follow her. Another worry was that should the car track be repaired, tourists would probably come this way.

When next day we returned to Rapid Rocks we were greeted by the shrieks of baboons; these were so deafening that we knew they must be present in large numbers. It was not long before we saw a great concourse of them. They were everywhere. Very soon Penny rushed up; she seemed to be terrified and followed us onto the plain before relaxing sufficiently to stop and drink. We decided to walk her back to the Ridge, hoping that she would remain there until the baboons had cleared out. Since it was too hot by then for her to walk the whole distance, Makedde and I stayed with her while Jock went back to camp to fetch a picnic lunch. Later we were glad we had done this, for twice Penny tried to slink back to the thicket belt which was still occupied by the baboons. Instead we persuaded her to settle close to us.

As it became hotter and hotter, I developed a splitting headache, and was bitten by several kinds of insect; inflamed tick bites in particular made me feel ill. Penny, as if to make up for my discomfort, frequently emerged from her spiky lair and rubbed herself affectionately against me.

On his way back to camp Jock had discovered a shortcut across the plain which reduced the trek to Rapid Rocks to only 10 kilometers. We asked him to wait in the car for us while we induced Penny to follow us to the Ridge. It took all my powers of persuasion and patience to get her on the move; this I did mostly by playing hide-and-seek with her. We reached the Ridge only just before dark. I gave her some meat and then went to the waiting car.

When we saw Penny again, it was at Karai. She came for a walk with us and showed great interest in a dwarf mongoose whose unmistakable whistles of alarm had given him away. Penny besieged the bush in which he was hiding; eventually the little fellow scuttled out, the leopardess following close behind him. Soon afterwards we heard him crying murder. Remembering the many mongooses I had had as pets, my sympathy was not with Penny, and I was relieved when she returned defeated.

My tick bites had now developed into red, leathery, inflamed circles the size of oranges and itched unbearably. Having in the past suffered from tick typhus, tick typhoid, tick fever, and relapsing fever, I was afraid that I might develop an illness, so I drove to Nanyuki where the doctor there prescribed Chloramphenicol capsules which, if taken early enough, prevent the onset of tick-borne illness. Thanks to this drug I escaped any dire consequences from the bites.

On April 20, 1978, Penny was again in oestrus and, as usual on these occasions, in great need of affection. I therefore urged Jock to build the holding pen himself. This had become all the more urgent because a cattle-raiding leopard was now available for translocation.

During the next five days we tried to keep Penny not only on the Ridge but on the slope facing Turkana Hill at the foot of which we sited the holding pen. Its distance from the Ridge was about 4 kilometers, so a leopard could easily cover it in a night.

On April 26 Jock drove to Nairobi to collect the leopard from the Animal Orphanage where he had been sent for three months after being trapped. He was believed to be 3 years old, and weighed 36 kilograms. In preparation for his journey to Shaba he was tranquilized with 0.75 cc of Sernylan and 0.75 cc of Sparine. He was also given an injection of 2 cc of Penbritin suspension and 2 cc of stress vitamin, sprayed with Malamite powder, and treated for a minor wound with Terramycin aerosol spray. Finally he was tagged on his left ear with a blue strip, no. 28. Then at last he was placed in the crate and set off on his nine-hour journey.

He arrived in camp at 6:00 P.M. and we took him at once to the holding pen, hoping to release him into it before dark. Jock had brought 6 kilograms of beef which I fastened to a rope, hoping that I would be able to move it about and so prevent safari ants from getting at it.

Penny at Elsamere, five months and three months old

Scent marking ("jetting") at nine months

Playing with Joy in the swamp, thirteen months old

A favorite game, with Makedde holding a rabbit skin

Chasing a rabbit skin, Bodech Mountain in the background

On a termite hill, Shaba Mountain in the background

Penny on Stonehenge Rock, fourteen months old

A good rest after climbing a tree

On their walks Penny always kept close to Joy

Penny on Karai Rock, seventeen months old

One of the occasions when Penny
had lost her radio collar

Makedde with the stick we used
to keep her under control, nineteen months old

Penny and Joy, Bodech Mountain in the background

Penny in a dignified mood, twenty-three months old

We placed the door of the crate in front of a door in the fence of the holding pen, after which we opened the door and waited in silence. Our wait lasted an hour and a half, by which time it was totally dark. Nevertheless we were able to discern the leopard when he ventured cautiously out of the crate. During the night it rained heavily, and I was glad that Blue Tag, as we had named him, had arrived before the downpour. Next morning we left him alone to settle in and went to visit Penny. Although on the previous day we had seen six lions on the plain between the Ridge and Rapid Rocks, our radio detector told us that Penny had gone back there. Since we could not drive across the soggy ground, we had a long and tiring walk before we found her hiding in the thicket belt. While I fed her I left the bag in which I carried the meat on the ground; she pounced on it at once and carried it off. Afraid that she might eat the plastic, we pursued her—she thought this a delightful new game and refused to budge out of the thicket belt, so we were obliged to return home defeated.

Next morning she was again at Rapid Rocks. It seemed that she had determined to stay there, while I was equally determined to settle her as close as possible to Blue Tag. Later we collected 5 kilograms of camel meat and drove with it to the holding pen. Leaving the car some distance away we approached quietly till through our field-glasses we saw the leopard resting in the shade on one of the platforms.

When he saw us he made one leap the whole length of the cage and crashed against the wire while giving frightening growls. Four times he flung himself ferociously against the wire, then crouched in a far corner, ready for another attack.

I took the opportunity to close the door of the section he was in and to place the meat in the shade in the other section. At this moment Blue Tag hurled himself with such fury against the wire that separated us that I was quite frightened; it also made me aware of the remarkable way in which Penny was able to control such power, with the result that except for a few accidental bites she had never hurt me.

We spent all the afternoon trying to induce her back to the Ridge, a task made more difficult by the fact that when playing hide-and-seek with us, Penny often climbed a tree which enabled her to spot our hiding-place. When we reached the Ridge we found it invaded by baboons, and had to make a long detour before we felt we could leave Penny in safety for the night. By the morning she had moved, and was now much farther from Blue Tag; this match-making, though challenging, was proving most exasperating. I was nevertheless determined to succeed.

At midday we drove over to Blue Tag to give him another 5 kilograms of camel meat. By now he had been confined for three days, and the sooner we could release him the better, for his emerald green eyes expressed his growing rage as he repeatedly charged the fence. I dropped the meat, took a few photographs, and left.

While the bridegroom was bursting with terrific energy, the bride, when we met her at tea time, was yawning, stretching, and rolling around. She plainly wished to be left alone.

I did not want to risk a return to Rapid Rocks so I set myself the task of luring her to an area facing Blue Tag and eventually, by exerting a certain amount of patience, I was successful. I fed her and stayed with her until she relaxed, laying her head between her paws; then, giving her a last pat, I stumbled down to the car and drove at top speed to Blue Tag.

By the time we reached him it was dark. With only the headlights of the car to work by, it was difficult to open the door to freedom without risking being mauled; we did the job in complete silence.

During his captivity Blue Tag had had plenty of time to survey his surroundings and to decide whether, when the time came to make his escape, it would be in the direction of Turkana Hill or toward the bush-covered plain. I hoped he would choose the 4-kilometer run which would take him toward Penny, who must have seen our headlights and might already be on her way toward him. After we had opened the door we left, so we did not see what happened when he emerged from the pen; but next morning we found the bride still in the same place. She seemed apprehensive, and looked continually in one direction; she also made it plain that she wished to be left alone. After feeding her I drove on to the holding pen and found it empty. The meat I had brought was gone, and some feathers proved that Blue Tag had killed a bird which must have flown into the pen. Immediately outside the wire we saw hyena spoor, but further on the ground was so hard we had no means of tracing the direction which Blue Tag had taken. When we next saw Penny she was near the river at a place which was good leopard country. If Blue Tag had taken the shortest route to water he might have met her. I was encouraged to think that this could have happened when I saw that her head and collar were covered with mud. There was no mud in the area, so perhaps Blue Tag had licked her and there had been soil in his saliva.

All morning Penny walked in circles, listening intently and obviously anxious for us to go away. This was how she had behaved for a couple of

days, even carrying part of her meat into a bush from which earlier we
had heard vervet monkeys calling. As a rule these monkeys are silent and
only chatter when alarmed by a predator. This made us hope that Blue
Tag was nearby, a hope confirmed three days later by finding Penny's
collar again covered with mud. Then for forty-eight hours the radio
detector gave no signal and I was afraid that crossing the river she might
have been taken by a crocodile. When at last we found her she was
neither hungry nor thirsty in spite of the fact that she had had no food
or water from us for three days. She welcomed attention, and seemed to
be alone.

Next morning she reached Rapid Rocks, but two days later she moved
on a couple of kilometers to a rocky outcrop, which I called Far Rock. I
did not like this area for her; not only was the rock very close to the main
road from Shaba to the Samburu Reserve, but it was also near a spring
and a tourist site at the foot of Shaba Mountain across which runs the
southern border of the Park. Should Penny discover the formidable
massif of red rocks where leopards were known to live, we might lose her
for good.

Our next meeting was in a grove of acacia trees. Penny was more interested in gazing at the rocks below her than in the food I had brought
her. Hoping to prevent her from moving still farther away, we tried to
cajole her back to the Ridge, and succeeded in getting her to follow us for
8 kilometers, the longest distance that she had walked with us up to now.
Luckily the weather was overcast, for our journey took the whole day.
Before leaving her I stroked her, whereupon she jumped on my back and
bit my arm through my canvas glove. Perhaps she was expressing her
objection to being made to take so long a walk.

Makedde had gone to a funeral in Isiolo and I had been alone with
Jock. Now, assuming that the obsequies were over, I sent for him. He
returned, but was obviously upset. Sorry to have annoyed Makedde, I
stressed how dependent I was on him not only because he alone had a
license to carry a rifle, but still more because of his great knowledge of
the bush and of wildlife, and his understanding of Penny. Suddenly he
smiled, the characteristic twinkle returned to his eyes and he took a sniff
of tobacco—an old Turkana custom—before starting to tell a tale which
explained why he had been cross when I sent for him.

When an important member of his tribe is close to death, the relations,
even if they live 150 kilometers away, are summoned to comfort him in his
last hours. When the elder has been buried within his homestead, a very
fat sheep is killed; the fat is divided among the mourners, who pour it

ceremoniously onto the ground, and the meat is also divided into small pieces which are dipped in milk and placed on the ground. Finally, large quantities of water are poured onto the last resting place—to keep the elder cool.

When these rites have been completed the mourners return to their homes. A month later they come with their livestock and camp within a kilometer of the grave, each man kills five of his stock—goats, sheep, or cattle—and the company feasts for a week before going home. A year later this ceremony is repeated.

I asked Makedde how it was possible for so many people—they some-times numbered several hundred—to assemble with their livestock with-out interfering with the grazing and water rights of the local people. He replied that on such occasions, even if there was feuding between some of those involved, everyone cooperated; moreover the practice had the ap-proval of the District Commissioner.

Makedde told me that his early departure had given great offense, particularly since the elder, though in a coma, was not yet dead. He therefore asked to go back for four days; of course I agreed.

On the day Makedde left my new assistant, Paul Strickland, arrived. I had met him briefly a year earlier during his first visit to Kenya. Like many people, he had fallen in love with the country and its wildlife. He offered to help me with Penny. He was twenty years old and was study-ing zoology at the University of Alaska, but was prepared to cut his course short if I offered him a job. He had excellent references both as to his character and his abilities, written by a mutual friend whose judg-ment I respected, and I therefore engaged him.

When he stepped out of the car with not only the largest backpack I had ever seen but also with a guitar, I wondered whether I had made a mistake. Practicing in camp, let alone keeping a guitar waterproof, might present problems, but Paul looked so happy that I did not wish to dampen his spirits, so I only warned him that to keep a guitar in good condition would, given the extremes of temperature in Shaba and the great rains, be difficult.

Next day we set out to visit Penny but searched all the usual places without seeing a sign of her, nor did we get any radio signals. When the same thing happened again I became alarmed, fearing that she had gone beyond the range at which we could get a signal from the ground. In that case our only hope was to hire a plane.

I contacted a friend at Nanyuki who had a charter aircraft and he agreed to take us, but the plane proved to be a high-winged aircraft and it was impossible to mount a radio antenna on its wing. Paul had there-fore to hold the antenna through a hole in the wing, but to do this he had to press the 1-meter-long contraption against the fuselage. Though we did not know it, this actually made reception impossible.

Next we contacted Patrick Hamilton, whose plane had all the gadgets required for holding the antenna to its wing, but even this did not offer a simple solution, for its frequencies were different than those on our radio, and it would need the skill of several people to make the necessary adjustment. In any case Patrick Hamilton was not free to come to Shaba for five days. While waiting for his arrival we started off each day at the crack of dawn, investigating every likely hideout, creeping through dense bush where, unless we happened to be right in front of Penny, we could not hope to get a signal. Our attempts were unsuccessful.

On one occasion we stopped for a short rest near the river when out of it a lioness emerged. She was only 100 meters from us, and seemed as sur-prised as we were at our meeting; having taken a look at us, she trotted off.

On his return from Isiolo, Makedde told us that the elder was still alive, but that the mourning rites had been fulfilled so he could decently leave. Paul, Makedde, and I now explored new ground, climbing a hill just outside the Shaba boundary. This was the highest elevation we could reach on foot, and we hoped that from its summit we might get a signal, but all we achieved was a splendid view across the plains. They were dotted with Grant's gazelle and oryx and there was a herd of buffalo standing knee-deep in a swamp; there were ostrich too. On another day we followed the river downstream, scanning arid gullies and patches of doum seedlings, but our only discoveries were the bleached skulls of two baby elephants, one with its 1-inch-long tusks still attached. Once we almost stepped on a sleeping lion lying close to the river. Neither he nor the pride seemed to have noticed that we were nearby, unlike a herd of buffalo which thundered away in a cloud of dust.

At last on May 21, Patrick Hamilton flew in. He made a map of the area to which we thought Penny might have gone and which included three mountain ranges and 10 kilometers of the river which led to a coni-cal hill named Borji. All these were outside the Shaba boundary. Within 100 meters of the river, a spring formed a crystal-clear pool which was deep enough to swim in. It could be reached by a rough track made some time ago by prospectors digging for mica. Close to this track the river bubbled through extensive rapids; on its banks grew a belt of doum seedlings fringed by acacias.

As we flew over this area we suddenly received a strong signal from the doum thicket. Tipping the plane from side to side we flew so low that we almost touched the trees. I was very happy to know that Penny was still alive and safe from crocodiles.

We returned to camp to pick up the car and decided that we might need to sedate Penny to take her back to the Ridge. In case she had been injured, we also took antibiotics and a syringe as well as the Sernylan with us. We then drove 20 kilometers till we reached the turning to the mica track. After this we traveled over soggy limestone patches, passing many Grant's and gerenuk gazelles. This reassured me that there was plenty of prey for Penny—and Blue Tag, if they were together.

When we neared the rapids I called, "Penny, Penny, come!" and, as if she were already waiting for us, she emerged instantly from a doum thicket and walked right up to the car. Although I had not fed her for nine days, she was in perfect condition. She ate a few pieces of meat at some distance from Paul and Patrick, whom she watched suspiciously. This was the first time Paul had met Penny and I had asked him to let her take the initiative. Soon she moved to a bush some hundred meters away and lay down in the shade, waiting for me to follow her. I sat beside her and stroked her and she closed her eyes. There was a scratch on her collar, but nothing to indicate that she had been with a male except perhaps for the fact that she had a full belly. Was she now able to kill for herself, or had a mate, Blue Tag perhaps, helped to feed her?

While she dozed off I went to discuss with Patrick how to sedate her so that we could drive her back to the Shaba boundary before she decided to move farther off. Patrick thought we should leave her where she was, saying that he had noticed that our receiver was giving weak signals; he thought that we should get it repaired as soon as possible. Meanwhile he suggested we should try to keep in touch with Penny by calling her; for one thing if she had followed a male over a long distance, and he was still around, Penny might return to him even after we had moved her, and then they might go to some area where we could not trace them just by calling. Of course there was also the chance Penny might walk back of her own free will. This had happened to several leopards on which Patrick had placed collars. They had abandoned their normal territory for up to three weeks and then had returned.

By now it was very hot; the pool looked so tantalizing and so near that we drove over to it and had a refreshing swim among tiny fishes, just about 2 inches in length. The longer we stayed in the water the more fish emerged from the sedge-covered banks. They nibbled at us as

though they were hungry, and indeed I wondered how they could survive in this clear water. Many years ago I had found similar fish in another spring close to the Uaso Nyiro River. Later they were identified as
a previously unknown species of tilapia. No one could guess how these
fish came to that pool. Here at Borji the pool was on much higher ground
than the river, so, again, we were puzzled as to how the fish had reached
it. I collected a few, and after drying them sent them to Nairobi for
identification, but I received no reply.

We were happy to learn that the radio receiver could be repaired
within two days at Nanyuki, so we would not need to send it to the
United States. But while we were without it we must try nevertheless to
keep in touch with Penny, so next morning we started our search at the
spot where she had left us yesterday. We investigated the rapids and
realized that she could easily jump over to the other bank at this point,
but as there was no indication that she had done so we searched 4 kilometers up- as well as downstream, calling all the time and creeping
through thick, thorny riverbush. But after all it was only yesterday that
she had had to put up with a plane roaring low overhead and then had
been confronted by two strangers, so I did not blame her if today she was
reluctant to show herself.

Back at camp that evening I broke a tooth, so next day we skipped
our ill-equipped search and instead drove 200 kilometers to the Mission
hospital. In spite of her fragile and feminine appearance, the dentist
proved to be both extremely strong and skillful and deftly removed the
broken tooth which, to her surprise, had two roots instead of one. Apparently she had seen this only twice in thirty years of practice.

When I signed my name on the bill she looked at me and exclaimed:
"Oh, you are Elsa's friend! *Born Free* is one of my favorite books." Few
dentist appointments have ended with a more pleasant surprise than finding an Elsa fan in this unlikely place.

When we got back, the repaired radio receiver had arrived; properly
equipped, we could continue our search with better hopes of success.
Alas, we needed to get to the top of Borji before we were likely to get a
signal. I was reluctant to undertake the stiff climb, so Paul and Makedde
went up, returning triumphant to report a strong signal from the direction of the river. At least Penny was still about, but she evidently did not
want to join us.

Next day the men climbed Borji twice in vain while I waited halfway
up at an abandoned mica mine. Although there were still several rich
excavation sites with heaps of mica around, the digs had obviously not

proved commercially viable. On our way home we took more readings until, all of a sudden, we got a signal from the Ridge. Penny was home again!

It was late afternoon before the signals led us to her. We heard the excited chatter of vervets and then we saw a baby vervet clinging terrified to the top branches of a bush and Penny throwing herself at it in high, twisting leaps, clutching at the bush and trying to shake the poor little monkey to the ground. My mind flashed back to Elsamere where, as a small cub, she had gone into just such contortions to get at a rabbit skin which we had placed out of her reach. Panting and absorbed, she tried from every angle to get hold of the monkey until finally it fell down and landed in the middle of the bush within easy reach, but amazingly, Penny made no attempt to pounce; instead she watched it clamber slowly up again until it was safely perched on a top branch. Only then did she resume the chase, jumping at the bush, while the monkey hopped from branch to branch to keep its balance.

Briefly she came over to us, rubbed herself against me and even against Makedde, but ignored Paul whom she was meeting at close quarters for the first time. Though clearly famished and thinner, her coat had the usual healthy, bluish sheen. Her vulva was dark red instead of pale pink, so I hoped that copulation had taken place—in which case the male might also have helped to feed her. She was as trusting and affectionate as ever, but there was something new in her behavior, as though she had matured since we had last seen her. She wolfed the meat we gave her while keeping one eye on the vervet, and then returned to pester her prey.

It was the first time I had seen Penny hunting, and although I was glad she knew how to, my heart went out to the poor baby vervet who kept looking at us with his expressive eyes which seemed calm, even while his tail kept on trembling. We watched Penny's antics till it was almost dark but then we had to leave her still besieging the little monkey.

Next morning she was in the same place but there was no sign of the vervet or of any remains. She was very welcoming and was most anxious to be stroked and patted not only by me but also by Paul, whom she had completely accepted. She declined the meat I offered, which admittedly was slightly high, and just took a long drink of water. She joined us for a walk but it was not long before we met a troop of baboons. This meant that we had to hurry Penny off in the opposite direction so that she would be safe from their attacks during her midday slumber. We returned in the afternoon with a freshly killed rabbit which we put in the bush where the little vervet had been, interested to see how she would react to it. She tried to shake it to the ground, but when it fell she carried it under a bush to store it. Hungry as she was, the rabbit would have been wasted if I had not handed it to her. I wondered how she had survived the last two weeks if she had not been fed by a male and also why she clung to her infantile habit of only storing food. Next morning I tried a new experiment and gave her a big lump of meat instead of the usual cut pieces. She dragged it to the rocks and hid it before joining us for a walk. Why, since she was so clever at catching, killing, and eating birds did she not react in the same way to rabbits, which so closely resembled the hares we put up daily during our walks?

We were now in the area that Penny had frequented after Blue Tag's release and where she remained for three days. She was definitely alone, demanded far more of our attention than she had up till now, and was gentle.

Six days after her return from her two-week safari, we found fresh leopard spoors on the Ridge; they were larger than Penny's but we could not tell if they were Blue Tag's. We located her not far from them. Though she took a long time to respond to my calls, when she finally appeared she was unusually boisterous, thrashing herself about, dragging her hindquarters as if paralyzed, swaying as if she were drunk and growling all the time. She brushed herself against Paul and me, but if we tried to touch her she dashed away instantly only to return soon and repeat her strange behavior. It was when she was close to us that these odd contortions took place; once she was a little way off she moved normally and stopped growling. She had only growled twice playfully at Elsamere while still a tiny cub but those noises were very different from the present continuous, deep growls which sounded rather as if she wanted to tell us something. She never looked at the water, let alone the meat, but spent half an hour exhausting herself in this eccentric manner. Finally she had a long drink, and then carried off the big piece of meat in the direction from which she had come.

We waited for half an hour, expecting her to return, but she did not. Penny was now 21 months old. I had observed similar behavior by Elsa and other lionesses when they had been in oestrus and had submitted to a male, but Penny differed in that she dragged her hind legs and swayed from side to side as if paralyzed. She had been in oestrus several times before, so why did she display such submission rites today, and why to us, if a leopard was near?

By next morning she had walked about 8 kilometers to Far Rock. Before we reached this large outcrop we noticed vultures dispersing from a kill near its base. Soon afterwards we located Penny under a grove of acacias. As soon as we came near she repeated yesterday's antics: rolling and exposing her belly, growling, swaying, and dragging her hind legs but walking perfectly normally when out of our reach. This performance continued for half an hour; after that she settled down, drank a lot of water, and carried the meat off to store it under a thicket, while constantly looking back at the rocks and listening intently. I recovered the meat and handed it to her; she received it in a normal fashion, but as soon as Paul approached she started to growl and throw herself about. This was certainly not an aggressive display, for she already liked him very much. I now noticed that her vulva was discharging—she was in oestrus. What reason had she had to move this long distance to Far Rock? She followed us across a lava-strewn plain for 2 kilometers to the cliff at Rapid Rocks, repeatedly displaying to Paul while walking normally with me.

The following morning she waited for us near the cliff; again she displayed and submitted and refused water and meat. We had seen fresh lion spoor nearby so we decided to walk her back to the Ridge. Even after the long, hot walk, which lasted most of the morning, Penny would neither eat nor drink till we arrived at Karai and then she once more displayed to us.

Next day, in spite of our trying to coax her back to the Ridge, there she was, at the cliff. Once more before drinking and eating she went through her exuberant demonstrations. She seemed very restless and circled us continually, so we assumed that a leopard was near and did not stay long.

This recent behavior suggested that not only was Penny in oestrus but, judging by the three dispersals of vultures, that a predator was near. Since it was unlikely for her to stay close to lions, we assumed that a leopard had been responsible for the kills. In that case, why did Penny submit to us? I feared that I might have imprinted myself too much on Penny and unwittingly turned her into a neurotic animal, but when I called up Paul Sayer on the radio he was most reassuring, and told me that he had seen similar behavior by a leopardess at the Orphanage who had displayed to her previous owners, but was later found to be pregnant.

After eight days Penny appeared to be normal again, and was obviously alone.

CHAPTER NINE

Penny Goes Courting

I ASSUMED THAT PENNY was pregnant, and hoped to settle her at the Ridge for her accouchement because she would be less disturbed than at Rapid Rocks where there was a tourist track. There was also the possibility that she might cross the river to hide her cubs where we would not be able to help her in an emergency.

We maneuvered her once more to Karai, where she remained for four days. It was confusing to watch her jetting frequently on bushes on the Ridge to mark her territory, but never once doing this at Rapid Rocks, which attracted her more. Which of these two areas did she regard as her home?

Meanwhile there were five lions near the camp, all in an alarmingly emaciated condition. Moreover, we noticed that the lioness, a mother of four cubs of about 14 months old, had a badly injured front leg and was evidently unable to provide for her still dependent family. I recognized the pride from their previous visits to the swamp; they seemed to have accepted us as harmless for they let us drive within a few meters of them without moving.

I sent word to the Warden, asking him to bring a kill or to let us shoot a buck for the starving pride. For the next few days we watched them getting weaker and weaker, by now only able to drag themselves to the swamp for a drink. Finally one dawn we heard a feeble roar, after which they disappeared; when we got permission from the Warden to shoot a buck, we could not find them.

Other animals who lived around the swamp or whom we passed every day on our visits to Penny also seemed to have accepted us and never ran away, however close we drove. For instance, there was a family of wart-hogs who only raised their heads as we approached, instead of trotting off in single file with tails erect. Oryx and Grant's gazelles stood by the road, flicking their ears and tails. They either continued grazing when we passed or remained resting in the shade, preferring the clouds of dust which the car raised to moving off into the sun. Then there was a bull giraffe who got so tame that we could almost touch him before he ambled off, to say nothing of our herd of buffalo which emerged almost daily at sunset to drink at the swamp. Watching them grazing peacefully, silhou-etted against the setting sun and the wonderful colors of the evening sky which ranged from every shade of yellow to red and purple, was an ex-quisite pleasure. Later, when the sky turned velvet black and star after star came out we often saw satellites threading through the constellations or a noisy jet droning over, reminding us of a world so different from our own.

Not only the animals outside the camp were used to us, but the birds within it were now almost tame, so that we had to be careful not to tread on members of the youngest generation. We put water pans and crushed maize near our tents during the heat of the day. I could not fill them quickly enough. Often the birds sat so close to each other that it was difficult to identify the species, but the most dainty drinkers were the white-browed sparrow weavers, often bullied by the buffalo weavers and superb starlings. They competed with the very noisy queleas who gave way only to the Cardinal woodpeckers, and with the Kirk's francolines who claimed priority because of their size (that of small chickens) and their belligerent habits.

Two fan-tailed ravens were a great nuisance to the cook, poking their beaks into all the food as soon as he turned his back, while the white-tailed go-away birds behaved in a much more dignified manner. The water pan next to my sleeping tent was occupied by frogs. As soon as it got dark, they sat in it, half submerged, and croaked a lullaby which put me to sleep.

I never needed an alarm clock, for at six sharp each morning I was awakened by the first sleepy twitter of the weavers. Soon every bird in the vicinity contributed to the cheerful dawn chorus which welcomed the new day. After this, sleep was out of the question, and it was not long before we were on our way to see Penny.

In the dry season we could drive the first 10 kilometers, taking readings on the way until we located her. Sometimes it took half an hour before she responded to my calling and appeared either from the rocks or the bush; she was always pleased to see us. After rubbing herself against us she would have a drink before we set off on our walk. Makedde and Paul led the way while I kept close to Penny to watch what she was doing. She seemed to enjoy these walks as much as we did until it got hot; then, we found a shady place in which to feed her. After her meal she liked to be stroked by Paul or me, and to our surprise she began to extend these intimacies to Makedde who, hitherto, had rarely been allowed to touch her. Later she would walk away, making it plain that we were dismissed. She never wanted us to know where she spent the rest of her time.

Paul was surprisingly knowledgeable about East African birds, especially raptors, and I learned a lot from him; indeed, we had many other interests in common and this made life in camp more enjoyable.

One afternoon we counted no fewer than eleven lions resting in the thicket near the camp. There were six half-grown cubs, four lionesses, and one lion. They looked at us, and we watched them through field-glasses. Suddenly a bull, a cow, and a calf buffalo emerged from the bush no more than 50 meters away; they seemed oblivious to the lions, and stared at us for about ten minutes. Neither the lions nor we moved, and the buffaloes grazed on, now within 10 meters of the cubs.

We were spellbound, expecting a kill at any moment, but nothing happened. The cubs sank into high grass till only their ears were visible, but the adult lions remained in full view. The buffaloes went on munching and paid no attention to the cubs, who occasionally craned their necks above the grass to see what was going on. Then two lionesses came up to the cubs, and they all ambled their way to a little pool where they drank. Afterwards they climbed onto the tree which Penny had used as a playground. From this vantage point the lions watched the buffaloes moving about, apparently quite unaffected by their presence. They no doubt sensed that the lions' bellies were full and that consequently they were no menace to them. In the same way they seemed to be sure that we did not represent a danger. When the sun began to set, the last of the lions and buffaloes made their peaceful way in opposite directions. I was left with the thought that we had witnessed a scene that confounded the theory that the two species are natural enemies.

During the night Penny had apparently moved back to Rapid Rocks. We found her chasing a hyrax into a crevice; nearby were lion spoors, and in the sky eight egrets were dispersing after having, no doubt, been on a kill.

Penny moved on to Far Rock. This was in the opposite direction to that which the lions had taken. Since I did not wish her to settle in this area I led her back to the cliff, and there we found a shady tree beneath which I started to feed her. Two minutes later a tourist car approached along the track. We froze behind the tree; nevertheless, six pairs of binoculars were fixed on us, and we heard exclamations: "Look at that leopard! It's wearing a collar!" Penny stared at the people but remained immobile. This was the first time she had been confronted by a tourist car. I was glad to see that she never moved during the half hour that passed before they drove on. After this incident I decided not to feed Penny near the public highway.

She for her part took the precaution of crossing the river to territory where she was not only out of reach of tourists, but also of ourselves. We reckoned that she had crossed at the rapids, but I could not jump over the slippery rocks there and had to wait on the near bank while Paul and Makedde searched the far side. They were now in a prohibited military zone, but at the moment there was no activity going on there so they searched all day but without success. However, next morning we got a strong signal, and they followed it. It seemed as though Penny was deliberately moving away from us, for though they continued to get signals, they never caught a glimpse of her.

Paul and Makedde returned for lunch, and afterwards we set out to look for an easier crossing. About 2 kilometers upstream we came to a narrow gorge where the cliffs on the far side rose up in sheer walls of rock. Walking along for about half a kilometer we came to a place where the river went underground. A natural bridge formed by fallen rocks and boulders made it possible to get dry-shod from one bank to the other. Penny might well have crossed here.

While I awaited their return six hippos surfaced frequently in a nearby pool, snorting their protest at the presence of strangers. I wondered where they went to graze, and how these heavy beasts, who cannot raise their legs high enough even to step over a foot-high log, managed to reach the top of the gorge where we had recently seen their spoor.

The following day Penny was waiting for us near the cliff, swaying and growling just as she had done nine days earlier. She certainly could not be in oestrus again, yet for the next eight days she continued these displays, and was unusually affectionate. Our next sighting was beyond Far Rock, right on the main tourist road. It took a lot of persuading to induce her to walk back to the cliff, and the track she chose was a most circuitous one behind boulders and rocky outcrops which would make an ideal lair for her, well out of sight of the tourists. Great rocks had broken off and been shattered, their remains forming crevices, caves, and platforms. High up on the cliff was a narrow ridge which led into a cleft about 2 meters deep, and too narrow for a lion to get through. From here Penny would be able to overlook most of the valley, and observe the approach of lions or baboons. Moreover, the cleft was waterproof, and if she sighted danger approaching, she would be able to leap onto a nearby shelf, descend on the far side, and hide in the thicket below. She, too, must have liked this place, for she often led us there during our morning walks. On one of these occasions I photographed her stretched out on the branch of a tree, her long legs dangling down on either side. She looked relaxed, but looks can deceive, for she suddenly jumped at me, clawing at my arm. It was three months since she had hurt me, and I wondered whether this attack was due to her intense dislike of being photographed. The wound was not deep, but in the future I was very careful when photographing her.

Later the area became thick with smoke and we saw that grass fires were rapidly advancing toward the camp. Penny was safe enough on the Ridge, but we had to hurry home to cut firebreaks, and when darkness fell the whole sky reflected the deep red glare of the advancing conflagration. The situation was becoming alarming when some trucks full of Africans arrived. They had been engaged to beat out bush fires, and worked all through the night and on into the morning, while the police remained in camp to help us cutting firebreaks. By evening the wind dropped and it was possible to control the fires, which, we learned later, had been started deliberately by poachers. Both Tsavo and Meru had suffered severely from such fires.

In the morning we found the spoor of two cheetahs along the path at the top of the Ridge. Penny had returned to Rapid Rocks, possibly to avoid them. She was very playful and seemed to enjoy our company, but by the following morning she had crossed to the far side of the river though still within earshot. While waiting for her to come over, I watched the hippos, whose plump, glistening bodies rose at intervals out of the water, only to splash back after taking a quick look at us. They were about 10 meters away so I took a lot of photographs, but when a bull emerged and came straight at us we ran off as fast as we could, until we saw him go under again.

When we heard the alarmed chatter of vervet monkeys I knew that Penny was approaching. I put a new roll of film into my Leica, but before I had time to take any pictures I felt a nudge on my shoulder, and there she was. She was quite dry, so she must have crossed by the natural bridge, making a detour rather than to risk crossing where she might have met crocodiles or hippos. She seemed very happy and rolled and rubbed herself against our legs, while the vervets stood on their hind legs on the far bank yapping at us.

We then climbed a new outcrop from which we had a splendid view over a vast area, with rugged mountains, conical hills, and the palm-fringed river winding through the boundless plains. Afterwards we explored three caves connected by a tunnel and there found a few rusty tins of food indicating that it had been used by poachers. Penny played hide-and-seek with us, and showed herself very determined to keep out of our reach. We took the hint, in case there might be a male nearby, and left.

Next morning she came from the direction of Cave Rock where we had left her, and gave her submission display. On our way through the thicket belt we had seen many buffalo spoor and an egret acting as tick-bird to them, so we walked Penny in the opposite direction, to the far end of the cliff.

Paul and Makedde were ahead of Penny and myself, and had climbed the rock. Suddenly they beckoned to me in great excitement. They had in fact seen a leopard, but by the time I reached them he had disappeared, though on the sand below Paul and I clearly saw his pug marks. Neither of the men was certain whether or not this male was Blue Tag. We were surprised that instead of rushing after the leopard Penny followed us, displaying all the time, not to him, but to us.

We were now able to trace both their spoors together on the sand. She accompanied us to the car and watched us drive away; perhaps she had come to see that we really did go off, and that we were not going to interfere with her and her mate. That she had a mate seemed certain when next morning we found six bites around her collar. Growling and displaying, she let me investigate them. Two were in an awkward place under the collar, and were bleeding badly. It is well known that lions, cheetahs, and leopards end their mating with a gentle, almost symbolic, bite on the female's neck, as if to mark her as their mate, but these bites seldom draw blood, so I could only assume that the hard collar had impeded the leopard, and that in frustration, he bit more ferociously than he would normally have done. I washed and disinfected the wound with sulpha-nilamide, but this, unfortunately, was immediately rubbed off by the collar, making it more inflamed than ever. Moreover, after her night with the leopard I was astonished that she demanded more stroking than usual. She was reluctant to eat. It was the first of July which meant that, with a gestation period of ninety-three days, she might have cubs at the beginning of October. Now, of course, we knew that she had not con-ceived in May when she had been absent for two weeks, possibly with Blue Tag.

The following morning she waited for us at the base of the cliff, dis-playing vigorously, but during our walk looked around nervously. When Makedde heard a leopard cough not far away, we understood her rest-lessness and left. On our return we found the Warden waiting for us, and as it was Sunday we drove off to the waterfall and had a picnic.

With an improvised rod made of a nylon line attached to a doum palm frond, the Warden caught two barbels which were excellent eating. He had never been to Penny's Gorge and since she was nowhere near us that morning we took him off to see the place. He was impressed by the pic-turesque rock formations and by the number of hippos in the pool. We walked in silence; suddenly Penny jumped out from behind a rock, growling and submitting, even to the Warden. As I tried to divert her and lead her away from him I almost collided with a leopard who grunted and vanished before I could have a good look at him. Now Penny led me in the opposite direction, rushing between us and her mate, rolling, growling, swaying, and even permitting the Warden to touch her.

During the following days Penny ate very little but displayed a lot, especially to Paul. Once again we heard the leopard coughing, but eight days later he seemed to have left, and Penny was back to normal.

For several weeks I treated her neck bites with an antibiotic Riko spray which was the only way I could find to disinfect the wounds under her collar. It took three more weeks for them to heal.

After this we did not see her for four days and got no signal from her. She had obviously crossed the river, but it was now so flooded that the men could not reach the other bank. When at last we got a strong signal, we realized that Penny must be high up on the slope of Borji Hill. Two hours later we heard the alarmed cacklings of guinea fowl, and then saw Penny sitting under a bush watching us. She did not mean to swim across the flooded river; nor did we. As we had seen a large troop of baboons nearby, it was as well she remained where she was.

Next morning her signal came from 5 kilometers downstream, near the rapids. We went there and watched her pacing the bank, looking at us, and trying to find a crossing. She was too scared to jump over the rocks. Paul and Makedde decided to walk in full view of her in order to guide her to the natural bridge, and perhaps help her to cross it. Meanwhile I would drive the car as near as possible to the bridge.

I had made up my mind that I would never feed Penny on the far side of the river, for if I did she might move farther and farther north, well out of Shaba and into the military reserve. If the river flooded she would be hungry without our supplies, since it seemed that she could not yet feed herself by her own kills.

After an hour's wait by the bridge, the barking of baboons announced the approach of Paul and Makedde, with Penny a long way behind. The men had patiently coaxed her into the gorge and got her to jump from rock to rock while the river crashed around them. Penny was very frightened but she finally made it, and in a few moments she flung herself down next to me, asking to be stroked. Then she moved under a shady log and gobbled 1½ kilograms of meat as fast as she could. This time she had lost weight. Meanwhile large troops of baboons appeared on both sides of the river and barked at her so I decided to remain while Paul went back to camp and collected a picnic lunch, fishing tackle for himself and Makedde, and some of my proofs on which I could work while sitting in the shade. It was not long before we were comfortably settled under Boulder Rock with two ravens croaking overhead, asking for bits of my sandwich, and Penny resting close beside me, half asleep. Sitting there with my page proofs on my knee, I realized that publishers' deadlines seemed a far cry from my own unpredictable schedule.

The sky was now overcast, and as soon as Paul and Makedde joined us we set off for the Ridge. It was reasonably cool, Penny followed us amenably, and we left her safely at Karai. Here she remained for two days, during which she strongly submitted to Paul. I turned over and over in my mind the reasons for these infrequent sexual displays, for which there seemed to be neither cycle nor rhythm. She could not be in oestrus, she could not be attracted by another leopard, and it could not be a social greeting rite, similar to those of lion, wolf, and hyena who always obey certain formalities when rejoining their kin. My conclusion was that Penny's attentions to Paul were sparked off by the coincidence of his arrival at the time of her reaching maturity. One other possibility was that leopards might be inducive ovulators, but when I inquired the reply was negative—leopards could not get into oestrus whenever they saw a male. Penny may have taught us a hitherto unknown leopard habit, but it was baffling to be unable to say exactly what the habit was.

We tried our best to keep her away from the baboons, but she obstinately returned to Rapid Rocks in spite of the fact that they were still there. When we found her she submitted once more with continuous growling, and in half an hour finished a whole rabbit except for the skin. With this she teased us, obviously hoping we would try to take it from her. This had been a favorite game with Elsa and Pippa's cubs and had usually ended in a squabble. We did not rise to Penny's invitation and before long she carried her treasure off in disgust.

Next day again she submitted to us, all the while listening intently for some sound. Her face and upper lip were scratched and bleeding, which looked as though she had confronted a baboon; two days later she had two more small wounds on her mask and two bites on either side of her flanks. She was very exhausted that morning, and when some baboons appeared on the cliff she fled for cover into the thicket belt.

Two days later she had two more wounds in her left ear, and was decidedly subdued. Makedde's theory that these were only thorn scratches did not convince us; Penny had collected an unusual number of wounds in one week, and was now more nervous of baboons than she had ever been. Later we found the remains of a small baboon, fluff and flesh adhering to part of the jawbone, in the thicket belt which Penny frequented; and here for the first time I saw her marking her territory at Rapid Rocks.

We wanted to get her away from the baboons so that her wounds would have time to heal, so again we walked her to the Ridge, but she only stayed there for a couple of days.

The last two months of heat and drought had made the roads and tracks, especially those of the limestone plains, excruciatingly dusty. This dust was powder-fine and penetrated everything—radio equipment, cameras, car engines. Our four-wheel-drive Toyotas churned ever deeper ruts, and the heavy going increased the already prohibitive gas bills. At this moment I was offered on loan the Renault which the Elsa Fund had donated ten years ago to a research project. Since that was now completed, I gladly took the little car to help save the roads and economize on gasoline. It was instantly nicknamed "Dik-Dik" after the smallest antelope in Africa. Old and minute it might be, but it drove beautifully, sailing smoothly over the knee-deep ruts and dusty potholes; to feel as though one was riding on the back of a caterpillar was infinitely preferable to being bumped and jolted in one of the Toyotas.

At first Penny would not come near the Dik-Dik. This was a healthy reaction to an unfamiliar car. It was two days before she accepted it, and by that time she was once more in oestrus, displaying strongly to Paul. Makedde had gone on leave, Penny had crossed the river again, and it was dangerous for Paul to follow her alone, so we left her, assuming she was with a male. We decided to drive to Meru after lunch, and spend the night with Patrick Hamilton.

Next day Patrick was off to make an aerial census of the livestock of the Boran tribesmen who lived in a conservation area next to the Meru Park. The Kora Game Reserve, where George lived, was only just across the Tana River which was the boundary between them, and the flight from there to his camp only took ten minutes, so Patrick kindly agreed that we could charter his plane and see George after he had done his census. I was thrilled to have this unexpected chance for a visit, even if it had to be a short one.

Flying over the conservation area taking counts of camels, goats, and cattle was fascinating. At this early hour they were all still in their thorn-fenced *manyattas*, but looking at this parched and barren ground I wondered where these creatures could find enough grazing and water. While low over an outcrop we received a strong signal from one of George's collared lions which had been missing for three months.

When we landed at the airstrip which George had cut out of the dense bush, the first thing we saw was his notice nailed to a tree: it told visitors that lions had priority here, and that walking was not advisable. It was not long before George himself drove up; he was very surprised to see us, and delighted that we had located his missing lion. Before going after it and trying to bring it back he wanted to establish the whereabouts of two other lions he had not seen lately, so soon we were bumping off in search of them along one of the many tracks he had cut through the thorny scrub leading toward some not far distant rising ground. As we approached we saw it was a rocky mountain with a track winding up it such as only George would tackle. The gradient was at least 45 degrees, and we simply prayed that the brakes would hold. We reached the top without mishap and were rewarded by a splendid view across a vast expanse of bush stretching as far as the eye could see, with the Tana River winding through it; but, alas, even from this height we could get no reading on any of the animals George believed we might see, so we went back to his camp for a belated breakfast. We were not the only guests; we shared our meal with buffalo weavers and superb starlings who helped themselves from our plates while at least a hundred vulturine guinea fowl gleaned maize meal and millet from the floor. The tamest were five hornbills (von der Decken and yellow bills) who took peanuts from George's hand very gently, to the great annoyance of a few pied crows.

We had to leave at midday in order to be home before dark, which was very disappointing, since it meant we could not stay to see the lions arriving for their camel meat. They were fed outside the fence, and George, while having his evening drink, would watch them from a distance of only a few meters, but definitely inside the fence. The morning went by very quickly, but, short as it was, it had been most enjoyable.

The following day Penny was waiting for us at the cliff, very hungry, and no longer submitting, though in a most demonstrative and demanding mood. It was very satisfactory to find her so near, because Paul Sayer was arriving that afternoon. He had not seen her since bringing her to Shaba a year ago, and I wanted him to check up on her condition and possible pregnancy. He has an exceptional understanding of animals; Penny showed no objection to meeting him next morning, and even allowed him to pat her. He was satisfied with her in general, but could not ascertain whether she was pregnant.

As if to confound us all, Penny vanished. Next day we got a very faint signal from the big mountain, Malkagalan. This was outside Shaba and opposite Penny's Drop. Like Bodech, Malkagalan was a range of reddish rocky peaks breaking off in cliffs and precipices that were connected by a saddle. The saddle itself was further broken up by deep ravines and smaller outcrops, the nearest of which was within 2 kilometers of the river. At this point there were rapids that Penny, but not Paul, could jump across. As a home for a leopard there seemed nothing to choose between Bodech and Malkagalan, and Penny was investigating both. For three days she scarcely moved down from the saddle, and probably spent her time watching us from some comfortable shady vantage point, while we searched for her along the river in the blazing sun. In the last few days the river had risen so high that Paul could not even cross at the natural bridge in the gorge, and we got very worried about Penny till six days later she turned up at the Rapid Rocks with a full belly, looking very fit.

After five days of normal behavior she again displayed, especially to Paul, though demanding caresses from me too. Surely by now she had been with a leopard often enough to realize the difference between us and her natural mate! If so, why did she submit so frequently to us?

Difficult though it was for Paul and me to refrain from giving her all the attention she wanted from us, we decided to harden our hearts and be much more aloof in the future, especially when she was in season.

This resolution was sorely tried one morning when she appeared with the head and thorax of a hare dangling from her mouth. She carried it proudly a few hundred meters to show us her kill, then dropped it in front of us and looked up. I do not know which of us—Penny, Paul, or I—was most thrilled at witnessing the first occasion on which she had killed a hare. Quickly I collected my camera while she carried her prize off and put it under a bush. I fetched it and put it in a good position for a photograph hoping that Penny would come out and grab it, but call and coax as I would, she refused to budge. She just looked reproachfully at me as if to say, "Why do you interfere with my kill?" I abandoned my efforts and gave the hare back, then sat close and watched her licking her blood-stained paws and face, rolling, growling, and displaying to us, very pleased with herself.

We started on our routine walk, wondering if Penny would follow us, but she stayed behind; when we returned after half an hour we found her with fresh blood on her paws and face, so she had evidently continued her meal in our absence.

After a fortnight, Makedde returned. The reason for his departure was that he had recently acquired a third wife for whom he still owed a few camels, so for the moment he couldn't remain in Shaba. With his concurrence, Ikeru, one of George's retired game scouts, agreed to join us for a few days to see how he and Penny got on, and if all went well, to settle his affairs at his *manyatta* and replace Makedde temporarily.

Ikeru was the tallest Turkana I had ever seen. This had earned him the nickname "Mrefu," the Swahili word for tall. (It was a great privilege for me to be allowed to address him thus, as it was one that he only extended to good friends.)

For his first meeting with Penny, I suggested that Mrefu should wear a pair of Makedde's trousers so that his leg-gear at least would be familiar to her. At first she was very nervous of him, and all she would risk after a two-hour walk was a cautious sniff.

Next day she was across the river once more. This was not in reaction to Mrefu's presence, for her spoors were found together with those of a male leading toward Bodech. Then Paul and Mrefu spotted her and her companion; at one point the leopards were within 30 meters of Paul but they kept running up the mountain, so, not wishing to chase them farther away, Paul and Mrefu returned.

We assumed that Penny would now spend a few days with the leopard, which would give Mrefu an opportunity to go home to sort things out. Paul took him in the car, while Makedde and I went to see if Penny had returned. We found her waiting at the cliff, very hungry. During our walk she frequently submitted to Makedde. Reserved as she usually was to Makedde, she preferred him to me if Paul was not present. It baffled me why she should leave her mate when she was in such need of affection.

On our way home, I added one more item to my list of baby-sitters, as I called any animal or bird I saw guarding more than three young. So far my list had consisted of giraffe, ostrich, impala, Grant, and chamois, but today I saw an adult oryx looking after six young.

During the night Paul found a spitting cobra in his tent. The cobra is a snake of great beauty, brick-red in color, with a black band 2½ centimeters wide behind its head; but it possesses a deadly weapon, the venom which it spits most accurately into the eyes of its victim, often permanently blinding him. This one we dispatched before she could spit, and the men scattered ash around the tent in the hope of deterring further unwelcome visitors.

We could get no signals from Penny the next day, and were roaming through forbidden territory searching for her when we passed an immature tawny eagle sitting on a tree. To get a good photograph, Paul had to get out of the car and squat on the ground in order to see the bird silhouetted against the sky. No sooner had he got to his feet after taking the photograph than three lions appeared not more than 20 meters away. They had been feeding on an oryx kill which we could not see from the road. It did not take Paul a second to jump into the car, at which the lions sneaked off in the opposite direction.

We had to wait three more days before getting a signal from Penny, who was high up on Bodech—farther than she had yet been from home. There was no water up there, and nothing to attract her unless she had company. Since August she had been across the river several times, probably with a male, and frequently submitted during those periods, but whether or not she had conceived we could not tell. When she turned up at the cliff after an absence of four days, we took her a good meal, but instead of appreciating our concern, she bit me on the arm without the slightest provocation. My left arm was by now a patchwork of scars, and this latest bite, though not serious, was a reminder that leopards are unpredictable. Penny was no exception.

❖

CHAPTER TEN

❖

Honeymoon

THE NIGHT MREFU arrived to replace Makedde, a puff-adder, one of the deadliest of snakes, was found by his bed. The Turkana was familiar with such hazards, and was not at all upset, but I insisted that the staff should remove their food from the sleeping tent into one which we set up a little distance away, for food attracted mice, which in turn attracted snakes.

I had to admit, however, that it was not only the staff's larder that was responsible for the arrival of the mice; the food I gave birds close to my sleeping tent was also responsible. I therefore set some traps, but to my horror one of my favorite crested francolines got caught by the neck. With its head upside down, it thrashed about wildly. I released the steel trap instantly, expecting the poor bird to drop down dead. Instead it walked a few steps, then ran, and finally flew off. Two days later it reappeared none the worse for its horrifying experience, the only trace of which was that its neck feathers stood up like a ruff and the bare skin below bore a scar. From now on it came daily to peck at the maize I scattered; previously it had always been one of a small flock, but now it came alone. Naturally I removed the trap and resigned myself to putting up with mice and even with snakes.

Penny was alone with her leopard for two days and then we found their spoor right on the main tourist road close to Far Rock. They were heading for the twin-peaked Shaba Mountain. This large rocky massif was far more dangerous than Bodech or Malkagalan because the southern border of the Reserve ran between the two peaks, and the plain below was thickly populated with both Boran and Turkana tribesmen and their livestock. If Penny got near these tribesmen and their animals she wouldn't live long.

There was a government embargo on all shooting of wild animals, and on selling game trophies; nevertheless, poaching was both widespread and profitable. It now appeared that the leopard was to be taken off the list of endangered species and would become open to all forms of commercial exploitation. With the words of the old Isiolo Councilor in my ears, I wrote a protest to the authorities. A few days later a group of American journalists visited me, which gave me an opportunity to explain to the press how important it was that the leopard be protected until a new census of the leopard population of Africa provided reliable figures. I emphasized that to do otherwise was to expose the animal to certain extinction and I asked them to give the situation publicity.

Next day Penny was near her cliff again, alone, and no longer in oestrus. Her honeymoon had left her with a bleeding gash on her forehead and two smaller wounds above her eyes, so no wonder she was anxious for attention. She was not thin after her three-day absence, but that did not prevent her from making short work of 4 kilograms of meat and marrow bones.

Next morning we gave her a rabbit, hoping it would encourage her to hunt hares. She hurried it off to the nearest shady tree, and then took a long time to decide where she could hide it from the baboons, who had now turned up and were squatting on nearby rocks. Eventually she raced off up the cliff to a cave that no baboon could squeeze into.

We wanted her away from Far Rock, which was infested with baboons. They watched our meeting in silence, which was strange because usually they made a tremendous hullaballoo when they saw us together. Once again we walked Penny to the Ridge, and she hurried along quite willingly in spite of the heat. Surprisingly, she remained there for eight days and appeared very content to be in her old haunts again after an absence of six weeks.

The familiar environment seemed to trigger off memories of long-forgotten games that she had played here with Martin. She was still very nervous of Mrefu, being, as always, shy of accepting a newcomer. He showed not the slightest fear of her, though he regarded the leopard as the most dangerous of all wild animals. The lion, he said, was a gentleman, and easy to understand; he told us he had speared several, something he would never dare to attempt with a leopard for he claimed to have seen a leopard slashing the throat and eyes of one man, and scalping another.

It was now nine days since Penny had submitted, and it was therefore no surprise to find her next morning on the other side of the river near Rapid Rocks. She was lying under a bush gazing at Bodech and only turned her head briefly when I called. Next day, when we found her at the cliff, she was in oestrus again. She seemed alert, but joined us only reluctantly for a walk during which she submitted to Paul. She made even stronger displays on the following day. A herd of elephants had passed, and their spoors and droppings marked their trail from the river toward Shaba Mountain. To the best of my knowledge, this was the first occasion that Penny had met elephants. She now rolled in the dung, biting at it and playing with it till she was muddy and reeking.

The following day, Paul went to Isiolo and I set out with Mrefu to look for Penny. She was waiting at the cliff, and seemed bewildered at not seeing Paul. She spent most of her time rolling in elephant droppings and finally, since her need to display to a male was stronger than her nervousness of Mrefu, she turned her attention to him.

We left her, well fed and tired, at Boulder Rock, but we had hardly gone a kilometer down the track when we saw a lion resting under a bush by the roadside. He raised his head sleepily as we passed, then continued his siesta; later we saw his spoors superimposed on our morning car tracks.

We had now been in Shaba for more than a year and it was delightful to see how placidly all the animals, with the exception of elephants, accepted our presence in the bush. We had seen a herd of elephants only once and they had charged us at sight. Apart from this we had twice heard them near the camp and had also from time to time found their spoor near the river. In view of the prevalence of poaching in the district, their wariness was very understandable.

Next day, for the second time, we found fresh leopard spoors leading from the thicket belt to Far Rock; hitherto the spoors had always led into Shaba from across the river. It was not long before we got a strong signal from Far Rock, together with loud lion roars, while the pug marks we saw indicated that four lions had moved in our direction and at least one very large one had gone off to Shaba Mountain. Penny's signal came from the summit of Far Rock, so we hoped that she was not only safe but with a companion. It has been supposed that in the cat family the female looks for a mate when she is in season, but in this case it was the male who had to catch up with Penny while she was still in oestrus.

We got a strong signal next day from the same place, so we took it that they were still together, but that very afternoon I saw fresh leopard spoors not 400 meters from the camp. I checked through my notes and established the strange coincidence that it was one year ago to the day— September 21—that a leopard had killed the Grant's gazelle near the camp.

Next day we got the same strong signal from Far Rock, and suspected that Penny might have gotten her collar off. The men struggled up the rock to look for it, clinging to overhanging boulders and scrambling along narrow ledges till they disappeared over the top of the cliff. At the base I found Penny's spoors, together with those of another leopard, leading along the Loop toward the river gorge. There I lost them on the rocks; on my way back I met the men triumphantly waving Penny's collar. It was now a matter of luck whether we ever found Penny again, but at least we knew she was with a mate while in oestrus.

On the following day I called and called, but in vain, though we saw the spoor of a single leopard coming from the river, with those of a cheetah nearby. I always enjoy reading the "daily news" freshly printed in the sand, telling us whom we might meet and whom we should avoid. Mrefu and Makedde were experts on this subject and could tell within minutes the age of a spoor, whether it was male or female, and if the animal were running or relaxed. We expected Penny to turn up soon, since we knew she had now been deserted by the male and would there-fore probably be hungry. Sure enough, there was a rustle in the grass and a panting Penny was rolling at our feet. I was sorry that I had no camera at the ready so as to get a picture of her without her collar. Paul quickly replaced the collar while I distracted her by stroking her. I was amazed that she was willing to tolerate the collar, which weighed 1 pound and was as hard as wood, but she did not seem to mind it. She was very thirsty and had lost weight since we had last seen her, so we gave her a good meal and left her at Boulder Rock.

We went to Isiolo next morning and when we returned we found a troop of vervet monkeys tame enough to come inside the camp enclosure to eat the dried acacia seeds which the surrounding trees had scattered everywhere. With the increasing heat and consequent scarcity of food, the three dik-dik who were our neighbors had come close to the fence to stare longingly at the few green plants in Penny's boma. I left the door open for them, but the vervets, who were quicker and tamer than the shy little antelopes, scampered in and ate the lot.

Waterbuck, Grant, gerenuk, and oryx now came more frequently to the swamp, which in turn led to the arrival of lions whom on most nights we heard quite close by. While we in Shaba were enduring the drought, up-country the rains were falling and the river was often in flood. We walked Penny to the Ridge so that she would be less likely to be caught on the wrong side of it and she settled down happily to hunt the plentiful hares and birds.

Once while we rested under a tree, I placed my hat high up in its branches, well out of Penny's reach. When she awoke from her midday sleep she spotted it at once, but made no move until I spoke; then she leaped up and shook the tree so violently that my hat came down, where-upon she carried it off with an expression of triumph.

On a cool but overcast day Penny was always full of energy. On one such occasion she jumped at me and bit my arm. The wide gash she had made needed to be stitched, so we drove to the nearest Mission hospital, 30 kilometers away. Unfortunately the doctor was on leave, so we had to continue for another 60 kilometers to Wamba, where the same Mission had recently built a large, well-equipped hospital.

In the past George and I had often camped in this lovely area. He was then engaged in the control of marauding elephants and lions. At that time Wamba was a tiny market center which served the local Samburu tribe; now I could hardly recognize the place. The main road was flanked by tiny wooden shops, and there was the hospital with 150 beds set in a bright garden which would have been the pride of any city.

I had to have a local anesthetic while my arm was being stitched up. During the operation I sang folksongs I had heard long ago in Italy; the Sisters, all of whom were Italian, joined in.

It was late in the afternoon when we returned to the camp. As we approached it we observed the tall figure of Kano, one of our workmen, walking toward us. He was dressed in his Sunday best, and armed with a panga. We asked him where he was going and he explained that when we failed to return at midday, he had gotten worried and had set out to look for us. I was touched that he had risked walking by himself through country full of wild animals to rescue us should we be in trouble.

The following day Paul had to go to Nairobi for a few days, so Mrefu and I were left alone to cope with Penny. Because of my bad arm, I was worried in case she should be in a jumping mood. I found that when I kept close to Mrefu she kept her distance, but if we were separated, she at once tried to jump at me. I felt that however playful her mood, it might end in another bite, so I drove to Isiolo hoping to persuade Makedde to return at least until Paul came back. I was lucky, for I found him at home and ready to help me, even though he had arranged to go on safari for a week.

Near Makedde's house I met one of George's former game scouts, Jiba, who used to accompany me on my expeditions in search of plants and insects. When he was with me I knew that I was well protected, and feeling relaxed, could concentrate on my work. Now he was so pleased to see me that he twice spat at me. As I knew this was the greatest sign of affection that anyone of his tribe could offer, I did not flinch. I also renewed acquaintance with our old driver, Ibrahim; this was a sadder occasion, for he had become not only very old but also completely blind and deaf. When he understood who I was, he shook both my hands and told me how much he missed the good old days.

On my return I was very glad to have both Makedde and Mrefu, for Penny was still liable to jump at me, but she obeyed Makedde's forceful "No!" She was by now very good at spotting prey and I realized that feeding her was not only unnecessary but was retarding the development of her hunting instincts; yet food was the only lure with which we could get her back when she had crossed the river.

After Paul's return we met Penny on her way back to Rapid Rocks. The ground had been churned up by buffalo and Penny made the best of it, rolling in their pats. She had now been on the Ridge for nine days and was not in oestrus, so presumably she was not seeking a mate. I wondered therefore what the attraction could be. Some days later we got a strong signal from a small rocky outcrop near the main tourist road. Hitherto, as far as we knew, Penny had never been there, but recently a leopard had visited it twice. After more days had passed, Paul cautiously approached the rocks. He put up a leopard only 20 meters ahead of him, which ran off with Penny in hot pursuit. It was not possible to tell if he was Blue Tag; however, we optimistically decided to call the outcrop Wedding Rocks.

For the next three days the pair appeared to be spending their honeymoon there. When we next saw Penny she seemed tired, dragging herself from one shady bush to another, yawning constantly; then she entered a ravine so overgrown with spiky doum palm seedlings that we could not follow her. Later, when she emerged, she walked with us, though reluctantly, and then suddenly uttered a strange sound, a high-pitched, whining chirp. I found it appealing. While she gently prodded Mrefu she repeated this sound several times. It almost seemed to me as if she wanted to communicate something to us.

She was very subdued, and had a bleeding wound above one of her eyes. This made us think that she might have mated. So I marked October 12 in my diary in red ink. If she had conceived, she might bear cubs in mid-January.

After she had had her daily ration she still seemed hungry, so Paul went back to camp to fetch a dead rabbit. When he left Penny disappeared, but the moment she heard the sound of the returning car she emerged, took the rabbit into the rock cave, skinned it, and then came out to eat it in the shade.

For the next week Penny waited for us almost daily. I sketched her several times but, as usual, she turned her head away, so I could only draw her full face when she was dozing. Later we saw the spoor of two leopards crossing the river by the natural bridge, and found Penny on the far side. Forty-eight hours later, she went up to Shaba Mountain into new country.

We were able to follow along a muddy car track which wound around the foot of the mountain. Here we came to some impressive fragmented cliffs with a few trees growing out of the crevices and got a strong signal. We called, but Penny did not answer though she must have been quite close by. We were 17 kilometers from camp, that is, halfway between Far Rock and Shaba Mountain, so we named the place Between Rock.

Close by was a forest of acacia trees—perfect leopard country teeming with Grant's gazelle, oryx, gerenuk, and hares; there was even a spring nearby, and the forest with its thick undergrowth was not frequented by baboons, who prefer rocky terraces. Hoping to keep Penny in a safe area, we decided to feed her only when she was near Between Rock.

We saw her five days later; she looked well fed but had a new bleeding wound on her forehead which I treated with an antibiotic Riko spray. She was full of mischief and climbed every tree with branches large enough to bear her weight; she allowed me to remove the ticks that had punctured her skin, and kept placing herself in positions that made it easier for me to find them.

CHAPTER ELEVEN

A Disappointment

A TOOTHACHE HAS to be attended to even if one is in the bush. I was suffering acutely, so I made an appointment with a dentist in Nyeri. He had finished and we were ready to go home when the car would not start, but after a bit of fiddling we managed to crawl to the local garage. It was booked up for repairs, so we had to risk the long drive to Nanyuki, only to be told when we got there that the starter motor needed to be replaced and that this would take two hours. We were doubtful whether we could now reach Isiolo before 6:00 P.M., at which time the barrier closes the road to all traffic heading for the sparsely populated territory in which Shaba lies.

Our fears proved justified, for when we reached the Isiolo barrier it was down. I spent another two hours persuading the District Commissioner and various police officers to allow us to continue our journey. Eventually we were permitted to do so, but only on condition that we pick up a Ranger at the gate of the Park who would escort us to camp and protect us from any dangerous animals that we might meet on our way.

We set off thankfully, but came to a halt a few kilometers down the road because of a flat tire. While we attended to this, the jack broke; there was nothing for us to do but wait, probably till morning, for a car to come by. We had not eaten all day and were very hungry, as well as tired. Mugo, the driver, stretched out on the back seat and I squeezed myself behind the steering wheel on the front seat. It was much too hot to close the window, and as a result, we were devoured by mosquitoes. At about one o'clock I saw the headlights of a truck; it pulled up and we learned that it was driving the 250 kilometers from Marsabit to Isiolo by night to save the tires from the noonday heat. The driver helped us to change our tire, and by 2:00 A.M. we reached the entrance gates to the Shaba Reserve. Since everyone was fast asleep, we decided to curl up again in the car and wait for morning. I tried to sleep, but Mugo's snoring and the whining of mosquitoes kept me awake.

When the first birds began to twitter, we went to collect Mrefu from his *manyatta,* which was nearby. A few grass houses stood on a treeless lava plain surrounded by a thorny fence placed there to keep the lions out. Since he had retired from the Game Department some twenty years ago Mrefu had lived in this place, existing solely on milk, tobacco, and a drug called Muraa. He used up his pension and any small sums he might make by selling an occasional goat to acquire this drug.

Muraa is made from the fresh leaves of *Catha edulis,* which are either chewed or boiled like tea. The drug is much used by local Africans. At first it has a stimulating effect, but soon produces a state of lethargy which lasts for days. During the colonial regime several attempts were made to discourage the use of Muraa but these had failed. Then a delegation of Somali women demanded its ban because they declared it made their men impotent. After this the sale of Muraa was forbidden, but it proved impossible to suppress the many surreptitious ways by which it was traded.

Judging by the many puddles we saw, the rain must have fallen continuously since we had left for Nyeri. Mrefu advised us to drive along a side track because the main road was likely to be under water. We took his advice, and in a little while sank up to our hubcaps. We were now stuck in a place where no one was likely to pass us. Gallantly, Mrefu offered to walk to the camp for help. This would take him a good five hours through difficult country, but since he had what I could only call a second sense for bush tracking, and carried a rifle, I thought he would be safe. All the same, I have rarely waited so anxiously for the sound of a car approaching.

It was 3:00 P.M. by the time I was put out of my misery by the arrival of Paul and the cook with shovels, a winch, and an axe. This was good, but they brought food and drink as well, for which I was truly thankful.

❖   ❖   ❖

Our daily walks in Naivasha

Makedde, please play with me!

Learning to climb a tree, eleven months old

Penny and her bat-eared fox (it was found
close to Elsamere, run over by a car)

Having been used to drinking from a basin at Elsamere,
it was difficult for Penny to learn to drink from a swamp

One of the many gorges along the Uaso Nyiro river

Penny on an ancient lava cairn, twelve and a half months old

Enjoying a roll in buffalo pats

Penny inspects Joy's offering

Tug of war

Listening

Exploring new territory, thirteen months old

Joy holding cobra, 194 cm long

On our next trip to Penny, we saw three lions, and met her only a few hundred meters farther on. She did not seem nervous and for the first time marked her territory near Boulder Rock. I sat down to sketch her but she knocked me over, sent my easel flying, and carried off the box containing my painting gear.

After an uneventful week, Penny again crossed the river to a cliff called Opposite Rock. We got a strong signal from there, but when she eventually scrambled down the steep rock she proved to be extremely hungry. While feeding her, I dressed her head wounds which had been scratched open. As I was doing this, I heard a leopard cough not far away and when Penny had had her fill she joined him. This time she neither displayed nor growled as she had previously done when she was with a leopard or in oestrus.

It is generally believed that once a leopard pair has mated and the female has conceived, the male deserts her. This made me wonder why Penny was still seeking the company of her mate. When she had been with him three weeks previously on Wedding Rock, she had been in oestrus, but today there was no indication that she was in such a state.

Our next news of her was from the Ridge, which was about 4 kilometers away. This was the first time that Penny had gone there on her own initiative. We thought she must have been following a male. Later we spotted her on the rock, but when I called her, she disappeared. We circled the rock as quickly as we could, and again heard the coughing of a leopard. We then made a detour to reach Karai Rocks; Penny had always regarded this place as our rendezvous, and she did so today. She was extremely hungry, and disappeared while still chewing the last piece of meat. I was now confident that she trusted us not to interfere when she was keeping company though we were still prepared to feed her when she was hungry. Next morning she appeared from the same area near Karai; her head wound was again bleeding and had flies buzzing around it. No doubt because they irritated her, she had been scratching the wound. Quickly she finished the 2 kilograms of meat and then moved some hundred meters away, watching us constantly. As soon as I had taken a second lot of meat to her she vanished without eating it. We waited half an hour then I collected the meat, whereupon she reappeared, rubbed herself against me, and was gone. A deep growl coming from the distance told us that she was still with a leopard.

As we returned to the car we noticed a troop of about 150 baboons approaching the Ridge. This may have been why she ran away from us, crossed the thicket belt, climbed over the cliff, and finally ran across the plain and up Opposite Rock. I ran after her, panting and calling. It was then that for the first time I saw the pair together, moving fast to the top of the outcrop and out of sight. I was not close enough to see if the male was Blue Tag.

By next morning Penny had crossed the river but, hearing my call, she suddenly leaped between the sheer walls of the gorge onto a pinnacle; from there she made a 6-meter jump across the precipice. On landing she found nothing to grip, but managed to raise herself to the height necessary to continue her flight till she reached a safe landing. She ate a lot and was very affectionate. Next day we did not see her so we supposed she was still with the male.

That night a herd of elephants surrounded the camp and churned our water supply into a bog. The 40-gallon drum which we had used to line it with had been tossed around till it looked like a concertina. We did not get much sleep, for to the loud trumpeting of the elephants was added a chorus of roars from nearby lions. This bedlam of noise was, however, more pleasant to my ears than the roar of traffic.

At our next meeting, Penny for the first time stored a rabbit we gave her in the branches of a tree. She remained close to her larder for a quarter of an hour, then followed us a few hundred meters to the car. We waited a little, expecting to see her return to her "kill," but she remained with us, so eventually we went away and then returned stealthily on foot to see if she were once more guarding her larder. She was not. She had remained where we had left her. Storing their food in trees in order to keep it safe from predators is characteristic of leopards, so why had Penny not returned to her "kill"? There was no ready answer to this question, and what made her behavior even odder was that there was a nest of tawny eagles nearby whose anxious parents would be looking for food for their young.

Weekly, we fetched our supplies from Isiolo; this time Mugo had gone off for them. After twenty-four hours he had not returned. On our way to Penny we met a Ranger who told us that Mugo had given him a lift to town, but on their way back they had been "taken by mud" and that Mugo was now with the car waiting to be rescued. We set out at once to find him. He was bedraggled and subdued after a sleepless night in the car, which was firmly embedded in the mud. While we were unloading it, Penny suddenly appeared, but kept off the track and under cover. Very likely she had heard the car yesterday, but only when Paul and I appeared did she feel safe enough to come into the open.

She now followed us to Far Rock where she remained. Her wound had nearly healed, and she was very playful. For a week after this we did not see her, but got readings from Shaba Mountain and later from Bodech Hills, which were some 10 kilometers apart, and between which the river ran.

When Penny next appeared she looked fit but tired; she was exceptionally affectionate, rolling on her back and nibbling her hind legs. My time with Elsa and with Pippa had taught me that these cats show no signs of being in cub until the last twenty-one days of their ninety-three-day pregnancy, so if leopards follow the same rule, and if Penny had conceived in mid-October, she would now be about halfway through her time. Since she was roaming about over a wide area, I wondered whether she might be instinctively seeking a suitable nursery for her cubs where they would be safe from baboons and other predators. Perhaps it was wise for her to do this early, before she was handicapped by advanced pregnancy. As the days passed she became less active and seldom moved during the night; she also avoided the sunshine and rushed for shady places; she drank much more water than she had up to now, and preferred the bones I gave her to be mashed up. We also noticed that she had become very jealous; when Paul and I talked to each other she tried to attract our attention, and demanded that a fuss be made of her. In view of all this Mrefu was quite sure she was pregnant, and he bet me twenty shillings that she would bear her cubs in mid-January.

The rains had turned Shaba into a paradise of flowers, and I was astonished to see how many I had never observed before. Our long walks to find Penny were hard going, but we botanized enthusiastically; within half an hour of rain falling, buds could change into fully open flowers, which added interest and excitement to every expedition.

Every day at the same place we met a friendly golden jackal pup. He was most inquisitive, and came right up to the bumper looking at us with the innocent and trustful expression common to all young animals who have not yet met danger. Where, I wondered, was his mother? Nearby a pair of Kori bustards were courting. They puffed out their neck feathers as they strutted along, and the male turned his tail into a fan set at right angles to his body.

During the rains there was good grazing; the families of gazelle, gerenuk, and oryx had plenty of milk. Fawns abounded, and there were also piglets of all sizes. It was delightful to see all these youngsters hopping about and ignoring our presence.

I also observed a cheetah with two cubs. They were younger than those we had previously seen, so obviously they did not have the same mother. I wanted to find out how many cheetahs were living in Shaba, for one day I would like to breed cheetahs there as I had in Meru. Now that Penny never came near the camp there seemed to be no reason why I should not have both species simultaneously. On several recent occasions I had suggested this plan to the authorities, but so far I had received no reply.

Now, instead of following her custom of changing her habitat every eight or ten days, Penny stayed close to Rapid Rocks for eighteen days, then disappeared for twenty-four hours. When we met again near Between Rock she was very hungry and quickly wolfed all the meat except for one piece. Not wishing to waste it, I rubbed it around her lips and almost forced her to swallow it. When we left she was lying behind a bush and remained there until we were out of view. Then she streaked after us and knocked me flat. She had never done such a thing before, and I could almost imagine it was her revenge for being bullied into eating something she did not like. I was amazed at her strength; weight for weight I was heavier than she, but I could not stand up to her onslaught.

Christmas time had come again, and we were expecting friends from Cyprus to stay. Of course we would not be able to show them Penny, but at least we could show them the golden jackal pup, and, as it happened, one day we met his parents and two siblings who blocked our path. The youngsters rolled and tumbled and chased each other, entirely ignoring our presence.

Golden jackals are rarer than their silver-backed cousins. They seldom mix, so we were surprised when two silver-backs joined up with our family. I took the opportunity to photograph the group, which was lucky as I never saw any of them again. I was also able to show my guests seven lions on an oryx kill. Their bellies were so bloated that they did not move off for two days even though our car was parked within 10 meters of them. An average oryx only weighs about 200 kilograms so I could not understand how one such oryx could have fed a fully grown lion, a half-grown lion, four lionesses, and one cub to the point of satiety. The mystery was solved later when we found the remains of a Grant's gazelle.

For Christmas I had the usual tree improvised from a balanites seedling on whose thorns I hung many strips of bright foil—so many that one could not see the foliage. Beneath the tree I placed drawings I had done of the heads of various animals. These I painted in a red that contrasted well with the silver tree, which shone brightly in the light of the white candles I had placed around it. We spent a happy evening regaled by the cook's excellent dinner.

On Christmas Day, assuming that Penny was far away, I wanted to show my guests the picturesque area around Rapid Rocks, but no sooner had we reached it than Penny appeared. She looked suspiciously at my friends sitting in the car, drank a very little of the water, and trotted off into the acacia forest. Paul, Mrefu, and I followed her, and once she could no longer see the strangers, she came to us and was very affectionate. Now I saw for the first time that her belly was much heavier and her nipples dark red and enlarged. There could be no doubt now that she was pregnant, and I thought this news was the best Christmas present I could have wished for. We went off for a two-hour walk, intending to end up at Boulder Rock, but when we were nearly there we saw a lot of people watching us through field-glasses.

Since it was strictly against Park regulations to walk a long distance from the car which had transported the visitors to the Reserve, I left Penny in the charge of Paul and Mrefu and went up to the visitors. As soon as I was within earshot they began moving toward me, calling me by name and asking for Penny. I inquired whether they had permission to walk in this area. I made a note of the license numbers of the Land-Rovers, and later told our Warden about the incident. The infringement of Park rules alarmed him as much as it did me. Unfortunately there are plenty of self-styled wardens and also guides and drivers who, when they feel pretty sure they will not be caught, accept tips for enabling tourists to photograph animals they would be unlikely to see from the established tracks.

One morning, at the end of our walk with Penny, Paul climbed over the side of the cliff to collect something that had dropped from the car. Penny followed him slowly, her belly obviously very heavy. Suddenly I heard Paul yell, and baboons shriek. When he returned he told me that he had seen a large troop of baboons advancing along the cliff. His waving had frightened them, but when he had reached the base of the cliff, he looked back and saw Penny apparently oblivious of the presence of the baboons, who were very close to her but hidden by a rock. As he watched Penny clamber along he suddenly saw a big baboon chasing after her and coming up to within a meter of her tail. He rushed over to ward the baboon off, and the leopardess, now aware of the danger, ran for safety into the thicket belt. This was the second time she had found herself unexpectedly face to face with a large troop of baboons. Had she been aware of their approach, she would have made off instantly, since she was justifiably very frightened of them.

Next morning Paul and Mrefu had to drive to Isiolo, so the cook ac-

companied me on my expedition to Penny. When we came in view of
the cliff I saw more baboons on it than I had ever seen before. Penny had
waited for me hidden in high grass and at a safe distance from them. She
came out when the car approached but vanished when she saw the cook;
it was a long time before she responded to my calls and then she only
stayed long enough to wolf down her meat. Next day we discovered that
she had retired across the river for safety.

George now flew in for a few hours for a belated Christmas celebration.
We planned to have a picnic lunch down the river at a spot not far from
where we had last seen Penny. We had stopped the car for a few moments, to check on her movements, when suddenly she appeared. Not
expecting her to be on our side of the river, we had neither meat nor
water with us, so Paul went back to fetch her rations while we drove a
few kilometers down the river and had our meal. By the time he returned
it was midday, and very hot. We called Penny, and eventually she came
slowly into view. Having fed her, we coaxed her to Cave Rock where she
could sleep off her meal. She must have liked it because next day we
found her there. She was now slowing down noticeably, and often rested
during our walk.

New Year's Day, 1979, began with Penny leading us to the river. Six
days later we located her at the base of Opposite Rock. She had lost
weight, and had two bleeding punctures on her vulva, which was moist.
Were the punctures caused by ticks, I wondered, or had she had a miscarriage? We were heartened by the fact that she seemed well, ate 2 kilograms of meat, drank a lot of water, and had no temperature. While
feeding her we heard the yapping of vervets and noticed some vultures
on a nearby tree. This told us that a predator had recently made a kill,
so we walked Penny in the opposite direction. As we walked I watched
her closely; she seemed fit, and I could not see any symptoms to account
for the external bleeding, which soon stopped.

The next signal we received was two days later, and it told us that
Penny had crossed the river and must have walked a good 10 kilometers
away from us. When we went as near as we could to this spot, she appeared, walked slowly toward us, and then rested under a doum palm on
the riverbank. Since this was not far from the spot where we thought she
could cross over, we coaxed her and she followed us along the far bank,
moving slowly. Judging by her appearance, we thought she had probably
another two weeks to go. She showed no wish to risk a crossing either by
jumping or swimming, so we thought she could now only cross by the
natural bridge.

During the next few days we were out of touch, and then we got a signal from high up on Bodech. Paul, Mrefu, and I decided to climb Bodech in order to discover whether there was any water up there. While crossing the plain we saw spoor that was obviously Penny's. Paul called to her, but the signal from the receiver showed that she was running away from us.

Figures show that the highest mortality among all wild animals is during the period that the mother is obliged to leave her cubs in order to get food. When Elsa and Pippa had been nursing their cubs I had provided them with food and drink in order to insure that there was no danger of the young being deserted for long periods; and I had done this in such a way as to avoid ever touching the cubs. I now thought I would need to do the same for Penny.

Up to now I had never attempted to cross the natural bridge, fearing that I might damage my implanted hip if I fell, but now I felt that I must take the risk. Penny would resent Mrefu's presence, and it would be dangerous for Paul to go there alone. However, on my way to the bridge, before I had even reached it, I fell and injured my left knee badly. In the course of recent years I had suffered so many serious injuries, accidents, and operations that I had much difficulty in keeping my balance and controlling my movements when crossing rocky ground. In consequence I had often fallen, but this time the pain was exceptionally bad. Paul drove me to the Mission hospital at Wamba, where the nice Italian Sisters had recently stitched up my arm. This time the doctor diagnosed a fractured patella and put my leg in plaster from crotch to heel. He told me to keep the plaster on for a month. This was going to prevent me from being with Penny when she most needed help.

Paul searched for her for eight days, and then returned with the news that he had seen her halfway between the river and Shaba Mountain, that she was very thin, and that all signs of pregnancy had disappeared. She had growled and submitted to him, but refused to walk. He had sat beside her, stroking and feeding her till she fell asleep, then he came back to me without waking her. Penny must have lost her cubs.

Cast or no cast, I was determined to see Penny, so· we set off and found her near the place where Paul had left her. I noticed that her nipples were shedding dry skin and had reverted to their normal size and color; she had an inch-long wound in one hind leg which could have come from a fight with a baboon. Might this have caused her to miscarry?

For fifteen days we had looked forward with great anxiety but also with great excitement to the birth of the cubs. Now we were not only dis-appointed but wondered whether she would ever bear cubs. I called George over the radio and he told me that one of his lionesses had had a miscarriage but had later produced healthy cubs. We could only hope it would be the same with Penny.

CHAPTER TWELVE

Penny Extends
Her Safaris

MREFU HAD NOW spent five months with us and needed a break; fortunately, Makedde's honeymoon had left him nearly penniless, so he was glad to come back. For the first few days of the changeover, Penny was rather apprehensive, even though she had known Makedde since she was a tiny cub. After five days she disappeared and for three days we could not get a signal. Then we saw her on the far bank of the flooded river. She was with a male, certainly not Blue Tag; both looked at us, then Penny walked to the river, obviously considering coming over to us, but when she saw the raging torrent she returned to the male and sat down happily beside him. Both looked well fed. Eventually they walked slowly away. Next day we spotted her about a kilometer from the river on the far side. She was alone.

By February 8 she had not been with us for two weeks. We scanned the whole area with our field-glasses without success, when suddenly there was a swish: I turned around and Penny nearly knocked me down a precipice as she flung herself at my feet. I was horrified to see how emaciated she was; never before had she been such a skeleton. I gave her a piece of her favorite camel meat but she hardly looked at it before carrying it away for a short distance where she ate it very slowly. The next ration she carried still farther and did the same once more before scrambling down the rocks to the bottom of the gorge to have a long drink. While struggling up again she looked constantly at the opposite bank, from which we heard the distant yapping of vervets. I wondered whether the male leopard was still there and if his presence had frightened the monkeys. When Penny returned to us I offered her more meat but she refused it. What could have happened to her to be so exhausted after a short walk? And though she seemed starved, she refused to eat. I thought that perhaps in her present condition she could only digest a very small quantity at a time. Dragging herself along and often resting in the shade, she followed us to the cliff. It usually took us fifteen minutes to get there but today the walk lasted an hour. During this time Penny repeatedly gave a harsh, throaty growl and belched. When we reached the cliff she had a long drink but did not eat.

I left her resting beneath a shady rock, thinking to give her time to digest the small amount she had eaten. We returned at four and found her in the same place, very thirsty but not hungry. She carried off the small piece of meat we had brought her and took it to a nearby bush where she chewed it very slowly. I sat close to her; she put her head on my lap and soon dozed off. Whenever she opened her eyes I gave her a bit of meat; she was very affectionate.

Fearing that her condition might be due to distemper or feline enteritis, I examined her gums and her eyeballs and was relieved to find that both looked healthy. I took her temperature, which was between 103° and 104°; that is to say, not a fever. Her coat had its usual healthy sheen and there was nothing unusual about her droppings. What, I wondered, could have turned her into skin and bone in so relatively short a time? By sunset she seemed relaxed and we left her on the cliffs.

Next morning she was there and ate two good meals and walked with us for two hours, eventually disappearing in the direction of Opposite Rock. During the next couple of days we doubled her rations and by the third day she was back to her normal weight. Her quick recovery made me think that what she had been suffering from was dehydration. Makedde had once told me that leopards could go without water for six days; during this time they live on their fat, but once this has been reduced they quickly become emaciated.

After five weeks my cast was removed. While I still had it Penny had been very gentle with me and had reserved her ambushing for Paul. On the day I got rid of my cast Penny shed her collar. Paul had much difficulty in recovering it; it continued to give out signals but was lying beneath a large rock which had only a narrow gap at its base. Paul looked through it and saw that it led into a spacious cave. Here was another place safe from baboons, one which could make a perfect nursery for Penny's future cubs. This point was driven home to me that afternoon when we were approached by an excited group of tourists. They shouted that they had seen a large leopard in the area, and did we know about him? I said we knew nothing of such a leopard and drove off in the opposite direction and soon found Penny at the base of a cliff. While I was feeding her I heard a car approaching and through my field-glasses observed the tourists, following us. Paul rushed off with Penny and hid behind a rock while I remained in my car and ignored the tourists, who very soon left. We then relaxed, but next morning we spied the tourists hidden in the thicket belt not far from where we had been with Penny. To outwit them we now took her for such a long walk that they lost patience and went home. Of course we could not prevent visitors from searching for Penny, of whom they heard from the Rangers at the gate, but we never took her near the road on weekends or if we heard the vibrations of a car.

After spending eight days with us Penny went off on safari. All signals during the first four days of her absence were faint and came from an elevation as high as Turkana Hill, indicating that she was very far away across the river; during the next three days we could not get any signal at all. We thought she might be behind the Bodech massif, and that this was why we received no signals, so we decided to explore the area.

To do this we would need to drive for 60 kilometers into the military zone. Choosing a day when we knew there would be no mortar practice, we crossed the river at Archer's Post and drove along the road leading to Merti, a trading center some hundred kilometers away. The road cut straight through the prohibited area. Halfway there, Makedde remembered a track, used during the war, which led close to the base of Bodech. It was now so overgrown and full of ant-bear hills and fallen rocks concealed by high grass that we had great difficulty in bumping along. After two hours we were close enough to the mountain for Paul and Makedde to get out and climb a cliff. From its summit they received a strong signal from Lolkanjao, the highest mountain in the area. It lies about 25 kilometers north of the river boundary. The country in between is waterless scrub with a few rocky outcrops breaking the monotony of the plain. What could Penny be doing in this arid country? We decided to get as close to her as possible; after traveling another 10 kilometers along the Merti road, we took to the open bush and came to a point which seemed to be within 2 kilometers of the spot from which the signals came. Here we went across country till we were within 2 kilometers of the mountain.

Unfortunately by then it was nearly sunset and so we had to turn around and make for home; not, however, before I had called and called for Penny without any result.

On our way back to camp we met a British officer leading some of his troops to a training exercise. He told me that for the next two days the Merti road would be closed because of rifle practice. Fearing for Penny, I told him why we were on the Merti road and asked him to tell his men to look out for her, that she was easily recognizable because of her collar and not to harm her. I gave him my camp address in case he should have news of her. Hearing my name, he said that about twenty-five years earlier he had had drinks with George and me at our Isiolo home. He then pulled out his map and showed us a cart track which led close to Lolkanjao, avoiding the military zone; he also gave us the dates when the area would be closed because of military exercises.

The following day was Sunday and Paul and the staff went fishing. After a while, as he was returning to the car to collect some more hooks, he was suddenly ambushed by Penny who, growling softly, rubbed her wet body against him. Although she had been on safari for so many days she was not thin, but she did seem hungry. Paul had only a little meat with him which he had taken as bait for the fish. He gave this to her and then returned to camp to collect more. Penny must have walked the 25 kilometers from Lolkanjao during the night. I drove back with Paul and found her still on the rock. She wolfed 3 kilograms of meat, came close to me, and then settled down in the shade. I got out my paints and Paul rejoined the fishing party. Later the men returned with a catch of barbels and we set off for home. Penny came with us to the car, and then climbed into a tree, probably to avoid any close contact with the staff.

Since her miscarriage she had spent twenty-one days on safari and only thirteen with us. During the first two weeks we had twice seen her with a male, and during the last week she could have been with one. Her moist vulva and her growls indicated sexual excitement and gave rise to the hope that she had again conceived. Since she had been living for so long on her own, I was amazed at the gentleness with which she took meat from my hands, carefully licking the marrow from my fingers without ever harming me. She had given up ambushing me and seemed to get more fun from preventing me from photographing her, for whenever she saw me with a camera in my hands she sneaked under a log and looked at me with a most impertinent expression.

After eleven days, during which she only became nervous if we saw any fresh leopard spoor, Penny again disappeared. We noticed that she was keeping to a well-established predator's cycle: spending eight to four-teen days in one place, then moving elsewhere to allow her prey to come back to the area in which she had been hunting, and after this herself returning.

For the next four days Penny was far across the river, at the foot of Bodech, and we only got a signal when holding the antenna horizontally. This suggested that she was lying down but when this persisted for an-other day, and the signal came from exactly the same place, we knew that she had once more shed her collar. Paul and Makedde had a tough climb on Bodech to recover it. They did so, but saw no sign of Penny. Now there was nothing to do but make a daily tour of all her favorite places, carrying food and water and calling till she chose to turn up. But all we found was the spoor of a leopard leading into the gorge and cross-ing over the river, but not a sign of Penny.

On one of our searches we met three flocks of newly hatched ostrich chicks parading along the car track. They could only just manage to walk if the ground was level, so we had to drive behind them very slowly till the parent birds found a suitable spot to get off the track. To begin with there were fifteen in one flock, but they were an easy target for predators, and very soon there were only seven left.

About the same time a pride of twelve lions stayed near the camp for several days. The leading male had a strange appearance: his huge red-dish mane was quite out of proportion to his narrow, pitch-black chest, and this extraordinary coloring made him look as though he had been singed. He was plainly a responsible character for he took his duties of guarding the three lionesses and eight half-grown cubs extremely seriously.

After twelve days, Penny turned up. She had lost weight, but was no-where near as emaciated as she had been after her miscarriage. On the off-chance of meeting her, we had put a rabbit in the car, but we knew if we gave it to her right away she would whisk it off to some inaccessible lair and we would risk losing her again before we got her collar on. We therefore hid the rabbit. But Penny was very hungry; ignoring our caresses, she stood on her hind legs to look into the car, and made it plain that all she was interested in was food. However, our chance came, and as the collar went over her head she let out the strangest whimpering whine, as if she were remonstrating with us for our indifference to her clearly demonstrated need. During the next three days she repeated this whimpering whenever she wanted to be reassured, but she ate very little.

She was now more attached than ever to Paul, following him wherever he went and declining to eat if he were not close by. To her he was not only a male, the first consideration, but also a playmate, someone she could treat more roughly than she could me. Makedde too passed muster, and she would rub herself against him or poke at his legs. With Mrefu, the rapport was more tenuous. Paul was leaving us very soon to return to America, and Makedde wanted to go home for a few weeks, so I wondered anxiously how Penny would get on with Mrefu and possibly a new assistant, particularly if she were to have cubs.

After being with us for about ten days she again disappeared. We found her spoors crossing the river at the gorge and received good signals from the far plain, but then, for the next three days, she seemed to be going farther and farther away till we got only a very faint bleep from the direction of Lolkanjao. We did not want her to choose a spot on this distant mountain as her next nursery, though from her point of view, so long as there was water there, it would be a good place, inaccessible to us and to tourists. George and I had climbed Lolkanjao some thirty years ago, and had found water there in a rocky pool, but I didn't know if this was still the case. The only thing to do was to go and see. At the moment there was no shooting in the military zone, so we set off to drive the 80 kilometers along the Merti road to search for Penny and check on the waterholes. We stopped the car; Paul and Makedde climbed some rising ground till they got a signal from Bodech, indicating that Penny was already on her way back! Nevertheless, we continued toward Merti, until we came to a wide, sandy riverbed in which Makedde knew there were a few permanent waterholes. The river, Lodesia, was not on the direct route from Bodech to Lolkanjao, but it was still important for us to know of its existence.

We gave up the plan of looking for water on Lolkanjao itself for the present and retraced our steps to find Penny. We reached the cliff by 3:00 P.M. Here we had a surprise, for we got a signal not only from our side of the river, but from very close by. Since 7:00 A.M. Penny must have walked and covered a distance of at least 8 kilometers on a very hot day, which was unusual. We found her near the river, lolling on the branch of an acacia tree. She must have heard the car, as well as my calls, but she was too tired to move and remained on the tree till we were right underneath it.

We had brought enough meat to satisfy a very hungry leopard and Penny ate till her belly was tight as a drum, after which she retreated to a nearby acacia on whose branches she could stretch out comfortably. With her stomach bulging out on one side, and her legs dangling limply, she closed her eyes in bliss. I photographed this comic sight, but her sated contentment was to be shortlived. All of a sudden she sat up, stared at the ground, took a flying leap into the grass below, and rushed off after a young hare which she caught and killed with a single bite. This was the first time we had watched Penny make a kill. The whole episode did not take more than a couple of minutes; she returned proudly with the hare to drop it into the fork of her tree, after which she flopped down on a higher branch to make the most of the breeze. An African black kite was hovering over the tree hoping to snatch the hare but I had no intention of allowing the bird to steal it. I wanted to save it for tomorrow's meal, and try to stage a "kill" for Penny, so that I could film her storing food. Gently I picked up the hare.

The next morning I returned with it. Penny was still there, but when we gave her the hare she took it to a shady place and started to eat it on the ground. This was not what I wanted to film so I grabbed the animal from between her jaws and tossed it into a sunny patch, knowing that she would not eat it there. This time everything worked out just as I hoped. Penny looked at me in surprise, but followed me goodnaturedly, then picked up the kill and carried it up into the tree. I was pleased that she trusted me enough to allow me to interfere not once, but twice, with her predator's most deeply seated proprietorial instincts, those concerning a kill. I got some good pictures with a new type of film, supplies of which had arrived only the day before.

I also very much wanted to film her crossing the river at the gorge before the rains came. Though we had often seen her spoor near the gorge, we had never seen her actually crossing, so next morning we went to the river and fortunately found Penny waiting near the end of the gorge. We had no difficulty in coaxing her to the river and filmed her as she hesitated to approach its muddy bank and instead jumped up the neighboring rocks. While she had great fun ambushing us, Paul and I struggled along with the heavy movie camera. The beauty of the gorge would have justified filming it even without the presence of Penny leaping between its reddish cliffs and walking along its sandy beach till she reached a spot where hippos were wallowing in a pool. They knew us well enough not to be alarmed and only to heave their glistening bodies between ourselves and their cubs.

Unfortunately, with my steel hip, I could not cope with the two precipices which separated us from the natural bridge so I had to make a long detour and enter the gorge higher up. From there I was able to reach a platform halfway down the cliff from where I could film Penny crossing the bridge and climbing up the opposite side. She was following Paul and she must have been puzzled when he repeated the crossing to make sure I got a good shot. Near me was a large cave which, judging by the bones, dry hippo skins, and wood ash drawings on its walls, must have been used by poachers before Shaba became a Reserve. Penny seemed familiar with the cave as well as with one on the opposite side of the river where we had seen her twice. This gorge and the surrounding outcrops were a real leopard's paradise and Penny made the most of it. I could not wish for a better spot for her to give birth—my only anxiety was in case she chose the cave on the far side, which I could not reach.

She stayed with us for the next eight days, after which we found her close to the gorge, obviously intending to cross to the other side. We tried to coax her back to the cliff, but she did not want to come back with us. We walked along the river in the shade of many umbrella-acacias while Penny climbed first one and then another. She did not mind the movie camera being pointed at her, but when I photographed her with the Leica she gave me a long, scrutinizing look through half-closed eyes—a warning that she was displeased.

It was a very hot day, and Penny was not in an ambushing mood, but followed us slowly until we reached a densely overgrown lugga leading to the river. There she rested, panting, under a shady acacia, and watched me pouring water into her bowl. Both my hands were occupied. Suddenly she seized the meat bucket and shot off with it into the lugga. I called to Paul to follow her as I was anxious in case she might eat the plastic wrapping, but Paul was slow off the mark, so Penny had plenty of time to hide herself. It took him an hour's intensive search, hacking his way inch by inch through the thicket, before he almost stepped on her lying 2 feet from him. By then it was midday and far too hot to eat. The meat and its plastic were untouched, but the aluminum box containing bone meal had a hole bitten right through it. Tired out, Penny rolled onto her back and, with her tongue out and the nictitating membrane covering her half-closed eyes, she dismissed Paul. It had been an exhausting business recovering the bucket, but we could not help laughing at Penny's perfect timing—waiting till both my hands were full to dash off with it and wreak her revenge on me for using the detested Leica.

Having twice been frustrated in her wish to change her habitat, she now made good her escape. Next day she was far away in the direction of Shaba Mountain; we decided not to follow her in case she might be with a male. We did not mind her being in this area, so long as she did not cross the river, which, judging by the dark and lowering rainclouds, would soon be in flood.

That night we had 3 inches of rain; the whole country was turned to a swamp, and we had to wait till midday before the road had dried a little and we could start out on our quest for Penny. Search as we did, however, we could not get a signal.

It had been a long and tiring day and everyone went early to bed that night. No sooner had I tucked the mosquito net under my blankets than I heard a soft sound as though something were rubbing against the canvas wall of the tent. I switched on my torch and saw the head of a mamba peering at me from behind a metal trunk opposite my bed. I raised the alarm and everyone came running, armed with the forked sticks we kept ready for just such an emergency. This snake, the deadliest in Africa, dodged all our attempts to pin it down behind the head and kill it before it had time to strike. The poor creature must have been injured while it was trapped behind the trunk and now sticks were jabbing at it from all directions; nevertheless, it suddenly shot out at an unbelievable speed and disappeared under the canvas into the dark. As it did so we got a horrendous view of the monster: more than 2 meters long and as thick as a wooden tent pole. After that, and because snakes are always more in evidence during the rains, we kept on the alert; and during the next week we killed a spitting cobra, a saw-scale viper, and a hissing sand-snake—all deadly poisonous.

Some days later while on my usual stroll near the camp I surprised two lions on a kill. They bolted when they saw me. Their kill, a young Grant's gazelle, bitten through the throat, was still warm and otherwise untouched. As far as I knew, Penny had never tackled anything of this size before, and as the lions had abandoned it I could not resist stealing the carcass to try to teach her a lesson. We loaded it onto the car and drove off, hoping to find her. She was where we had seen her that morning, and there was just enough daylight left to watch her reaction to the kill. She sniffed at it excitedly, then as it was too heavy for her to carry, we took it into a thicket at the foot of the nearby cliff. There she licked and tore at the skin, but could not open it. I slit the stomach so that she could get at the viscera. By then it was almost dark, and we had to leave.

Next morning we found that Penny had dragged her windfall into an even thornier spot and was guarding it carefully. She had eaten part of the viscera and half of one hind leg. After a long drink, she danced around the carcass, begging for help in opening the stomach further. I did so, and while she licked the blood I tore out the liver, kidneys, spleen, heart, and intestines, which I wanted her to eat while they were still fresh. Once again, she was quite happy to allow me to handle her kill while she was actually feeding on it. As for the entrails, she sucked in the intestines and took all the rest from my hand. When she could eat no more, she stood over the carcass and then dragged it between her legs for about 20 meters to another thicket. I filled the water bowl as quickly as I could, but by the time I reached the place, she and her kill had disappeared. As our aim was to teach her to guard it, I left the water where it was and we went home.

At tea time we wanted to know how she was getting on; we spotted her scrambling down a crevice with a large fig tree at its base and giant boulders all around, which formed a narrow passage. From where we were we could not enter it, so we had to clamber around to see if we could reach it from the top. Paul went forward, wriggling on his stomach, and right at the end of the crevice he found what was left of the Grant's gazelle.

I wanted to try to record Penny dealing with her "kill," but it was impossible to get the heavy movie camera up to where Paul was, so I asked him to get the carcass out if he could and throw it down to me. He did this but Penny's reaction was too swift for me. In a flash she was on it, straddling it and hauling it as fast as she could up the rocks and out of sight. She then sat down, panting heavily. I had failed to get any pictures, but I was pleased that at least Penny was guarding the carcass for another night.

Next morning we could smell the meat long before we saw Penny bounding down the rocks, her face and chest covered with blood and her stomach distended. I had never seen her in quite such a bloated condition before. We enticed her to follow us and about a kilometer away we settled down on the shady side of Far Rock. Paul then went back to collect the rotting carcass, for we did not want its smell to attract other predators to her retreat. All that was left was the extremely smelly head and neck, half a hind leg, and the forelegs. Penny had consumed the rest: ribs, vertebrae, viscera, and all the skin. Sated though she was, she pounced on the remains and went off to the rocks with a lump of meat. We did not see her again that day, but the stolen Grant had fulfilled my purpose of teaching Penny to guard a kill for two nights and days, as well as introducing her to a new item for her menu.

Next morning her signal came from across the river, and we followed fresh spoors to the natural bridge. We were close behind her, but the river was swollen, and even Penny must have found it as much as she could manage to leap across the wide gaps between the rocks, with the water rushing between them. More rain was on the way, and we were anxious to get her back. The signal indicated that she was close, so I called and shouted while Paul scanned the far bank with field-glasses. Somehow we missed her returning, and only spotted her when she was right below where we stood. Then she climbed up to a level equal to our own and performed a leap which I had seen her make only once before: with all four feet bunched on a pinnacle of rock, effortlessly she took to the air and landed on our platform, dripping wet, but undismayed and delighted to be with us.

I had hoped that Paul would stay for at least two weeks after his replacement arrived, but the plan did not work out, so this was his last day at Shaba. As Penny followed him affectionately that morning I wondered anxiously how we were going to get on with the stranger who was coming next day. He was a middle-aged South African with a degree in engineering, long experience of camping, and he spoke fluent Swahili—qualifications which seemed to fit him for the job. Alas, their first meeting made it clear that he and Penny were ill at ease and that they were unlikely ever to have a good rapport. Penny kept farther and farther away from us and it was not long before she took herself off to the far side of the river. I saw no point in persevering so we agreed that the newcomer should leave as soon as I found another assistant. He came in the shape of Pieter, a lad of twenty-two, the son of a former Game Warden in Zambia who was longing to join us. He had a British passport, so there was no formal difficulty about his coming to Kenya. This time the meeting with the leopardess went much better. Penny licked his hands, took meat from him, and rubbed herself against him in the most friendly fashion, while he stroked her, delighted at his initial success; moreover, he had a natural affinity with, and love of, life in the bush, and his ambition was to become a Game Warden in Africa.

Pieter was an excellent driver, and two days later I sent him off with all the staff to do the weekly shopping in Isiolo while I went out alone to search for Penny. I had got some distance when a plane appeared and buzzed the camp. By the time I reached our airstrip to pick up the passenger the plane had left, heading for Meru National Park, which worried me. I thought George might be in trouble for I knew that he had recently been involved with a gang of poachers. I was surprised to find no one on the landing strip.

The Isiolo expedition got home at 5:00 P.M., just in time to see a

Land-Rover arriving with a large trapping crate in the back. The driver was Patrick Hamilton, who had visited us in his plane but had found no one at home. He needed help, for he had taken charge of an orphaned leopard cub.

CHAPTER THIRTEEN

Bala

THE CUB WAS badly hurt; our first task was to get the frantic animal out of its stinking prison and into Penny's boma. Patrick managed to sedate it by sticking the needle through a small hole in the bottom of the crate.

The cub had hurt himself in his efforts to escape from the trapping crate, chafing his nose to the bone against the wire; he had also two broken canines, an upper and a lower one. We dressed his nose and the wounds around his mouth with sulphanilamide powder and took his temperature. It was 104°, 2 degrees above normal. We then examined his broken teeth and took his measurements.

Next we put a bed of grass in Penny's traveling crate and, in case it should rain during the night, we lifted the cub into it and placed it in the boma near a trough of water which could be filled from the outside.

While we stood about waiting for the cub to come around I heard his story. His mother had been trapped because she had taken to killing livestock. (I wondered whether her depredations of domestic animals might not have been due to her home range having been taken over for agricultural development, thus depriving her of her natural prey.) The original intention was to keep her till her cub was caught; then, both could be transferred to a Reserve. However, the leopardess escaped before the cub was located and when he was, there was nothing to be done but keep him in a crate until a home could be found for him. The Animal

Orphanage at Nairobi was contacted but already had more leopards than they could feed and house; in desperation Patrick had come to us.

As the cub slept on, I thought about the reputation leopards have for killing wantonly sometimes up to twenty or thirty goats in one night. I believe this can be explained by the fact that all carnivores will instinctively chase and kill a running creature, so when a leopard finds himself in an enclosed area, surrounded by panic-stricken creatures, he will strike at any animal within reach. Is it not significant that there are no records of leopards killing wantonly in the wild? Because of this I think the view current among farmers—that "the only good leopard is a dead leopard"—is unfair to an animal that is not naturally vicious.

The cub came around in half an hour and showed none of the usual swaying symptoms; instead, he made a methodical examination of his new home. His coat was dark like a forest leopard from a high altitude—he was certainly a beautiful cub. Watching his movements and comparing his measurements with Penny's at various ages, we estimated his age at between 9 and 10 months. If so, he was too old to get imprinted on me; however, we could not be certain of his age because we could not tell whether his small teeth were deciduous or were his permanent teeth not yet fully grown. What was certain was that two broken canines would be a great handicap in hunting and even in chewing his food. For the moment we fed him on mincemeat.

We named him Bala, a sound easy to project over a long distance. Since the rules about keeping wild animals are so strict I asked Patrick to record that the cub had been given to me with the approval of the Warden of Mountain National Park, Nyeri, and the agreement of the Shaba Warden. I also arranged that on the following day Patrick should contact Paul Sayer in Isiolo and ask him to come out to inoculate the little leopard against feline enteritis and distemper. Before he left we minced up a kilogram of meat to which we added bone meal and Abidec vitamins together with salt and some liquid paraffin. This mixture we placed near the water trough, but during the next twenty-four hours Bala refused to touch it.

He spent the time on the wooden platform nearest to our tents. To encourage him to eat and in the hope of making friends, I spent an hour next morning inside his cage, keeping 6 meters away so as not to alarm him by invading his danger zone. As with small children, I believe that the initiative to make friends should come from them, not from adults. But Bala ignored me and never moved off his platform. Fearing that he must be starving, we placed the meat dish on a 2-meter-long plank of wood which I carried in my extended arms while walking slowly forward. I meant to slide the dish onto the platform, but as soon as it was within reach of his paws, Bala pushed it off the plank, growling fiercely. At least the meat was now where he could reach it should he wish to eat, but by 5:00 P.M. he had not touched it, nor had he left the platform. Hoping to make him associate meat with me, I showed him some fresh meat and placed it near the water trough. I then sat for half an hour inside the boma, but nothing happened, so I went for a stroll. When I returned all the meat had been eaten. We prepared another meal and left it in the same place; then, as it was getting dark, I went to my tent. Later I heard the sound of drinking. Bala must have eaten too, for by next morning the meat had gone. We minced up some more, and I sent two men to Isiolo to buy a further supply, for I could not feed two leopards on Penny's ration.

When they had gone I found myself alone in the camp. It was very quiet. Hoping that Bala would become more friendly, I entered his boma with a book, and sat 6 meters away from him, near the door. After a while some vervet monkeys approached and started yapping. Bala growled but did not move, so the monkeys lost interest in him and went off. After their departure he went to sleep. Three hours later I was collecting my sketchbook when Bala jumped off his platform, growled fiercely, and charged me. I barely had time to hold the book in front of my face, but he bit my right hand before I could reach the door. I could not imagine what had provoked this attack; yesterday he had shown no sign of resenting my presence. Moreover, during the hot hours wild animals are usually sleepy.

As I was dressing my hand I wondered whether I had been mistaken in attributing Bala's previously passive attitude to friendliness; perhaps he had been simply too weak, after his traumatic experiences, to show his hostility. Now, having been well fed, he had obviously regained enough vitality to rebel against my presence and his confinement. I realized that I had better make as little as possible of my wound, but insure that under no circumstances would we, or any member of the staff, enter the boma.

As I was cleaning up the bloodstains I heard a weaver bird making a fearful din and saw it flying up into a tree only 3 meters from where I was sitting. Immediately afterwards I saw a very large snake emerge from the long grass and make for the birds' water bowl. It looked like the one I had recently seen in my tent. I froze, hoping it would go away but instead it wriggled toward me. Unable to tackle it because of my injured hands, I stood up and shouted loudly, which sent it off.

Later, after the men had returned, I went for a short walk with Pieter. Suddenly we heard the loud trumpeting of elephants quite close to the camp; running back, we saw a herd of fifty or more making their way to the swamp. I was surprised that Bala, who had growled at the vervets, remained unmoved when the elephants passed within 20 meters of his platform.

If so far he had been idle, he now made up for this by his nightly activities, which consisted of removing the stones we had placed along the wire fence to weigh it down. At first I did not worry because I knew that the wire was buried at least a foot deep on either side; but as the cub's nightly operation continued and the hole became deeper, I became anxious, particularly because he was digging along the fence that separated his boma from the camp. I did not like to imagine what might happen if he should escape by night when the camp gates were closed and find himself confined among panic-stricken people. It was only after several sleepless nights that I relaxed by reminding myself that the camp was built on lava and that it would surely be impossible for Bala to dig a tunnel deep enough to make his way out. Soon we settled into a routine: the cub was busy during the night with his excavations, and we were busy during the day replacing the stones, using a forked stick with which to push them through the wire, while also placing very heavy stones along the outside of the fence.

After Bala had been with us for two and a half months he had grown into a beautiful leopard and was still totally wild. The broken teeth proved to be milk teeth and his permanent ones were now halfway through; we therefore hoped that we would be able to release him as soon as his hunting instinct had developed sufficiently to enable him to be independent.

We had learned from Elsa's cubs that the killing instinct in lions develops at the age of 18 months, though instinctively they can from the first take advantage of the direction of the wind and drag a rag under their bodies as they would later drag a kill. From Pippa's cubs we had learned that cheetahs need fourteen months to develop their killing instincts, though they, like lions, require another three or four months to survive alone. I hoped to learn from Penny how leopard cubs compare in this respect. As we did not know Bala's exact age, I had to rely on Paul Sayer's judgment as to whether he could soon be released and survive.

I had consulted all the relevant authorities about his future, and the consensus was that the best place for him to be turned loose was just outside Shaba, some 20 kilometers from our camp, near the Uaso Nyiro River. Here there were rapids across which he might reach the rocky hills 2 kilometers upstream, which were alive with rock hyrax; the plains around had enough francolines, hares, dik-dik, mongoose, ground squirrels, and jackals for him to hunt. Since these plains were uninhabited by Africans, he would not endanger human life or turn into a stock raider, so it seemed an ideal choice.

In preparation for his release, Bala had to learn to recognize birds, hares, and other furred creatures as food, and also learn how to kill and open them. We took the opportunity to try out the effect of one of Penny's rejected rabbits on Bala and were pleased when next morning we found nothing but two legs and the contents of the stomach. He had selected the two corners of the enclosure to drop his feces: two little heaps of excrement neatly covered with grass.

Bala gradually adapted himself to captivity or resigned himself to it, but he never became tame. He stopped digging by night and while dozing during the day he watched everything that went on in the camp from his screened platform. He accepted us as harmless and stopped charging when Pieter or I passed close by his boma, though he still growled when any of the African staff approached it. He no longer snarled when we filled the water trough and placed the meat near it, though he never allowed us to come nearer to him than 8 meters without charging. I kept all visitors away so that he would not lose his fear of humans before he was set free.

I felt very sorry for poor Bala, realizing how bored and lonely he must be. There was nothing we could do about this other than talk to him in a low and friendly voice and call his name, but this only made him turn his head away. The drought was increasing day by day, and the only excitement he got was from the arrival of a large troop of about a hundred baboons who came daily to look for the ripe seeds of the acacia which they relished, and to turn over stones in search of beetles and worms. They soon realized that Bala was no danger to them, and they teased him without mercy. I marveled at the dignity with which he ignored his tormentors, looking in the opposite direction while they barked at him provokingly until I chased them away. This was a nasty job because there were so many of them. They left a musky smell behind.

Bala's daily meat intake was 2 kilograms of fresh camel meat with all the usual supplements; he ate it long after dark, when all the camp lights were out. Later I would hear him pacing to and fro for most of the night, only retiring to his platform when dawn came.

When we had had him for three months, Paul Sayer and Patrick Hamilton considered releasing him. Though he was in excellent condition, they decided, after examining his teeth, that he was still too young to defend himself should a fully grown leopard attack him. We should therefore keep him for a further two months. They reckoned that he was now 9 months old.

I was very glad we were to have him for a little longer, for I had become fond of him even if we could not play together. Francolines had taken to using his boma as a chicken run, and I was delighted when during the following weeks he caught and ate two of them.

The country was now drying out alarmingly, but the rains would not come for another two months. Already there was nothing to eat but straw-like grass and brittle scrub and even animals adapted to desert conditions, such as the gerenuk and oryx, got very thin. Livestock was in a worse plight, with the result that even the prohibited zone was soon dotted with thousands of cattle, separated from Penny only by the river. It was a good thing that she remained on our side.

Although the area we had selected for Bala's release was infested with tsetse fly, it might not be long before desperate Africans brought their stock there, preferring to sacrifice a few to the fly than lose the lot from starvation. If this were to happen at the time we released Bala, he would be doomed. We discussed the situation with the new Warden of Samburu-Shaba and agreed that we should take Bala into the Samburu National Reserve.

Pieter and I drove the two hours to the Park and, with the help of the Warden, inspected a place close to the Uaso Nyiro River where there were large trees and excellent bushy cover with plenty of hares, dik-dik, and ground squirrels. On the other hand, it was only 5 kilometers from the Lodge, too close to tourist traffic as well as to six resident leopards who might resent his presence. In addition, livestock were now invading the Reserve without permission, and were exceedingly difficult to control. Therefore we had the choice between this area or the adjacent Shaba, where at least for the present there was no livestock or human interference. We decided to release Bala in Shaba.

Five months after his arrival at my camp, Patrick and Paul Sayer came to set him free. Patrick, who came by air, assured us there was no sign of livestock in the area. After making a reconnaissance we chose a place where a large acacia tree grew within about 5 meters of the river, which at that point was lined with doum palm seedlings that provided good cover. There were rapids close by which, while the river was so low, would be easy for Bala to cross and from the other side make his way 2 kilometers upstream to the rocky massif of Malkagalan, a leopard's paradise. On the other hand, if he went downstream, the Borji Hill was but 2 kilometers distant. There were not as many small animals here as in Samburu, but Bala could survive on ground squirrels, hares, mice, and francolines; and when he had had more practice, there were plenty of young Grant and gerenuk to be had on the plains.

When we returned from our search, Paul tried to sedate Bala by shooting the drug with a darting pistol from outside the boma into his rump. We waited till 3:00 P.M., by which time Bala should have been very sleepy, but he was still watchful whenever he saw Paul approaching; it was another half an hour before he became drowsy. Paul was always cautious in the use of sedative drugs. In this case the initial dose proved insufficient and the ordeal had to be repeated while the semiconscious and swaying Bala watched suspiciously and made it very difficult for the second dose to be administered. At last by 4:30 P.M. success had been achieved, and the cub could be weighed and measured.

Only now did we discover that three of his deciduous teeth were still behind the permanent canines. Paul believed that they would soon drop out and that their presence would be less of a disadvantage to the cub than keeping him confined for a further period, during which he would become more and more used to human company and could not start learning to hunt. We therefore decided to release him.

With Bala bedded down in Penny's traveling crate, we set off on our forty-five-minute drive. We reached the tree and placed the crate right under it so that the cub could climb up it if he wanted to survey his new home. We put his familiar water trough next to the crate and cleared the surrounding ground of grass and pebbles so that later on we would be able to see Bala's spoors. We also put a little meat inside the crate and a 4-kilogram lump on a branch out of reach of other predators. While he was coming around the cub was less likely to hurt himself inside his crate than if he were outside swaying and collapsing among the stones and scrub, so for the moment we kept the door of the crate closed. We attached a long rope to it which we flung over the branch. In this way we could open the door from a safe distance.

After half an hour Bala sat up quietly in the crate. We pulled the door high up into the tree—and he was free. But he did not move and like most captured wild animals, when faced with strange surroundings, he remained inside the familiar crate until he felt safe enough to leave. We waited in silence till darkness fell, and then returned home. Not 4 kilometers away we saw a lion stalking Grant's gazelles.

At dawn we returned. Bala had gone. He had touched neither the meat in the crate nor the piece on the branch, and, as we had feared, it was impossible because of the hardness of the ground to see any spoors, so we could not tell in which direction he had gone.

Birds of prey had already pecked at the meat and as we did not want other predators guided by them to the spot we took it away. Even if he were hungry and returned, Bala would not eat the meat till after dark, but in case he might feel the need of familiar objects, we left the crate and water trough to help him in his bewilderment.

Later that day Paul and Patrick went home, but we returned to the tree at sunset with fresh meat and had a useless look around for spoors. I called Bala in the usual way, but there was no response. When we got back to camp I opened the door of his boma in case his leopard's homing instinct should bring him back; the distance was only 20 kilometers and he might well feel hungry.

For the next three days we repeated our morning and evening visits to the tree, calling and searching, but as there was no sign of him we eventually took the crate and water trough home. Every night I listened for the vervets sounding the alarm to herald Bala's return, but when no water-lapping broke the silence for a full week I resigned myself to continuing anxiety. I knew it would be very hard for him to fend for himself, particularly while he still had teething trouble. All I could do was hope he would survive. I was very familiar with the gnawing pain which had to be endured after setting a loved animal free and never knowing what happened afterwards. This dreadful uncertainty is indeed a high price to pay for sharing the life of a wild animal, and Penny and Bala were no exception.

CHAPTER FOURTEEN

Penny Gives Birth

BALA'S ACTIVITIES HIGHLIGHTED the difference between this wild cat and our Penny, who was imprinted on me and who grew more and more affectionate as her pregnancy advanced. Her symptoms were the same as on the previous occasion: she was very thirsty, ate twice her usual ration, avoided the sun, and reduced her movements to a minimum. She resented Mrefu's presence, especially when feeding. Her coat was exceptionally silky, her nipples were enlarged and, if my calculations were correct, she would give birth within three weeks, on May 26.

I felt almost certain that she would make her nursery on the far side of the river, and since it was very hard for me to cross, the men placed large stones wedged securely together in order to form a bridge. There was only one place where Pieter would have to give me a pull. The work was completed just two days before the river came into flood, which did only slight damage to the bridge. I was worried, however, in case the river should flood again and separate us from Penny. We tried to keep her on our side by varying her habitat. Every two days we coaxed her into an area near Far Rock, one in which she had never settled though it contained dense bush and was an ideal playground. Having walked her there we always made a point of ending up at Far Rock, from which she could overlook a wide area and spot any approaching lion or tourist car.

On May 13 I felt for the first time a lump the size of an orange near her rib cage. Was this a fetus? She still had two weeks to go, and I prayed that she would not cross the river. What worried me particularly was that she had now been on our side for longer than usual. I was therefore relieved when she moved on to Between Rock, a distance of 2 to 3 kilometers from Far Rock. This was not near any tourist route, and the highest of the outcrops was surrounded by an acacia belt. On the few previous occasions when Penny had settled there we had not received any signals. Now we hoped that she had found a good place for giving birth. Every morning she met us at the base of the outcrop in what to her was a rocky paradise, but to us a rocky hell.

Together we explored the nearby bush and acacia forest, always ending up on the rocks of this outcrop. Three days later we received a very strong signal but there was no sign of Penny. When Pieter climbed up he found no leopardess, only her collar wedged in a cleft near the summit. We suspected that there were caves close by which would make ideal nurseries.

For two days we searched and then met Penny at Between Rock. She was very thirsty; the nearest water was at the small swamp site, a two-hour walk—a lot for her in her present state. We decided that we must organize a water supply in a *karai,* as we had done at the Ridge many months ago. I hoped that Penny would give birth here, for it seemed to me a perfect place and unlikely to be frequented by baboons, for to reach it they would have to cross thick bush, something they dislike doing.

Penny ate and drank more than usual while cutting her exercise down to a minimum. She was very affectionate, licking Pieter's hands and behaving as though she wanted my support, very much like a daughter who needed her mother's company as her hour approaches. On May 25 at about 9:00 A.M. when the sun was already very hot, she climbed up some rocks, looked back, and waited for me to follow. I could not do so, but Pieter struggled after her till they both disappeared. The next thing I knew was that Penny was sitting beside me asking to be stroked.

Later I lunched at the Samburu Lodge with old friends of mine, Marlin and Carol Perkins. We have many mutual interests and have often met both here and in the United States to discuss questions related to preserving wildlife as well as their popular TV program, "Animal Kingdom." Today the conversation centered on the recent discovery of a living king cheetah, a species known to have existed in the past and to have inhabited South Africa, but which was generally believed to have long become extinct. The king cheetahs differ from other cheetahs in that they have solid black stripes along their spines from the root of their tail to their shoulders; and instead of spots, they have linked irregular markings all over their bodies except for the head, which is almost white. Hoping that Marlin might be able to stimulate interest and raise funds through his TV programs, to help discover more about these beautiful cats, I invited them to come to my camp next day so that I might show them a recent report on the fascinating king cheetah.

On our return we went to meet Penny again. We watched her stumbling down the summit toward us. Her belly was enormous and her teats looked ready to burst. I stroked her but did not feel the movement of a fetus. Later she went off, but waited at intervals for us to follow her and gave that very rare faint chirp that seemed to me an effort to communicate something special. I could not follow her over the rocks, but Pieter did; he was away so long that I became worried. When he returned he said he had had a very remarkable experience: Penny had led him to a rock with a small overhang. There she lay down, and he settled close to her, using her as a pillow while she licked his face and hands. Their rapport was complete. The sun was setting and on the horizon its rays were reflected by the glaciers of Mount Kenya, while in the foreground the bush faded to a warm glow in which the silhouettes of Bodech and Shaba Mountain stood out, as though floating. Pieter had evidently been deeply moved, and only when it got dark did he make his way back. Penny followed him until he told her to stay, a command which she obeyed.

As I expected the cubs to arrive at any moment, I started off early next morning. When we approached the area where Pieter had left Penny the night before we got a strong signal from high up on the outcrop. Since she might be in labor I did not call her but walked silently along the foot of the hill, carrying meat and water in case she should appear.

After half an hour we saw her coming slowly toward us. She was no longer pregnant; her vulva was covered with fresh blood and her nipples were sticky from having been suckled. She drank and drank, and seemed very tired. Of the pieces of meat I offered her she took only two, which she carried a short distance before eating. When, however, we produced a dead rabbit, she carried it up the rocks and out of our view. Later she came back and had another long drink from the *karai,* which I then placed as near as possible to where we thought the cubs might be. Afterwards she clambered up the rocks, obviously expecting us to follow. She seemed bewildered when we failed to do so, but I felt strongly that cubs so newborn might be too vulnerable for us to visit them yet. However, when Penny returned a third time, positively demanding that we should follow her back to her family, we gave way, justifying this on the grounds that she had now been away from her little ones for an hour, which was quite long enough.

We struggled over boulders and through vicious thorns till we reached a rock platform. Here Penny stopped, looking as though she wished to dismiss us so we took the hint and struggled down again. This time she did not accompany us.

I had been warned to be especially careful after the cubs had arrived for, like all cat mothers, leopards are supposed to be particularly danger-ous when caring for their young. Observing her behavior so soon after giving birth, I began to wonder whether I might not have made too good a job of getting imprinted on her, whether indeed I might not have done this at the expense of her maternal instinct. Even Elsa, with whom I had the greatest possible rapport, had concealed her cubs for a good six weeks; and Pippa had not let me see any of her four litters till they were five days old. The fact that Penny had kept closer to me this morn-ing than she had done recently might suggest that to her I represented "mother"—the supplier of food and security; she did not keep so close to Pieter, whom perhaps she regarded simply as a playmate. All three cats did have one thing in common: their objection to Africans approach-ing their cubs while they were small, though in normal circumstances they accepted old friends like Makedde.

Assuming that she and the cubs would stay for some time at Between Rock, which was 2 kilometers from camp, we explored the area and found an opening in the dense bush through which we could drive the car close to the outcrop. Next morning we approached the lair silently. Nevertheless Penny soon came down to meet us. She was very thirsty and hungry and gobbled up the meat we had brought, to which Paul Sayer had advised us to add 4 teaspoons of calcium lactate. Compared to its appearance yesterday, her belly looked more or less normal, though her vulva still had clots of blood on it. We gave her a dead rabbit, which she carried halfway up the rock; then she came back again, with the obvious intention of leading us up to the cubs. When we did not follow her she repeated the invitation. In all she spent half an hour with us, had a short walk, and then at last returned to her family.

On the third day, as Penny went on pleading with us to come and visit her babies, I thought it safe for Pieter to go up and locate the cubs and see if there was any path by which I could reach them. When he came back he told me that Penny had two cubs and had given birth to them at the place where he and she had rested the day before they were

Kula, the lion cub

Investigating a porcupine burrow in the gorge,
thirteen and a half months old

Drinking from a limestone crack—"Penny's Bar"

Unlike lions, leopards do not hold their food with front paws

Makedde and Kifosha cutting up a buffalo killed by lions,
Bodech Mountain in the background

Carrying the stick we use to keep Penny under control,
fifteen and a half months old

Bundling up

Biting hind leg before she jumps at us

Penny has ten parallel rosettes on her spine;
many leopards have only two or three

Queen of Shaba

Ready for more explorations

Penny still loves to be hand-fed
although she is now two years old

Out!

Natural boulder bridge in the gorge where we cross

Flooded gorge; the natural bridge is no longer visible

Penny pregnant, two weeks before giving birth

Penny at thirty-three months, with her cubs, three days old

Penny in the cave with one of the cubs, fifty-one days old

born. I was now determined that come what may, I was going to see the cubs, even if I had to balance precariously, jump across gaps, and try to hold on to rocks as sharp as a rasp. Pieter had difficulty in pulling me along where necessary while keeping an eye on Penny in case she might indulge in a playful ambush. However, she showed no intention of doing this but waited patiently, giving her low chirp as though to say, "You *are* going to have a surprise!"

At last I saw the two cubs. They were 7 inches long; their fur was dark gray and they were already spotted like an adult leopard. One was male and had parallel rosettes along his spine. Penny lay down in a position to be suckled. The cubs wriggled up to her nipples and, tiny as they were, fought for the teat with the best supply of milk, spanking each other while making a faint humming sound. Their eyes were still closed, their paws and mouths a dark red. They suckled until their tummies were like little drums, then they fell off and cuddled close to their mother. Young as they were, they kept on moving their tails. It is a characteristic of leopards that their tails are never still.

Penny licked them, looking at them with great tenderness; then suddenly her pupils narrowed to a pinpoint and her expression became murderous. At that moment I saw a hawk soaring high overhead. The overhang on which the family had settled was exposed to the sun and wind, and only just wide enough to accommodate us as well as Penny and the cubs. She looked very proud and dignified as she turned to lick our hands. As with Elsa's and Pippa's offspring, I was determined not to touch the cubs lest they should become imprinted on me. If I were to learn a lot about wild leopards from these cubs, I would be glad if they regarded me as a friend of their mother and therefore trusted me, but the last thing I wanted was that they should share their lives with me as Penny had done. I restrained myself from cuddling them with some difficulty, the more so because Penny was evidently surprised that I did not touch them. Soon they woke up and began to climb up their mother, hooking their tiny claws into her fur and heaving themselves onto her back only to roll over to the other side where her body sheltered them from the sun. Finally they settled between her forelegs, cosy and secure.

We stayed on, listening to the wind and the faint humming noise of the cubs. Below us lay the boundless space of the bush, and I felt as though I had entered a realm that but a few knew, for it existed only in dreams. It was hard to tear myself away, but it was getting hot. Fortunately I had my camera with me and was able to take photos of the youngest leopard cubs that I had ever seen.

Pippa had changed her lair every three or four days, so I thought that Penny might well by now have moved her cubs. Pieter went to reconnoiter and found the little ones still on the same overhang. He sat there for twenty minutes while Penny suckled them and licked his hand. When the sun got very hot, Penny suddenly grabbed one of the cubs around its belly and carried it away to somewhere shadier. The lair was exposed to the full sun so Pieter put himself in a position to provide shade for the remaining cub. After a quarter of an hour Penny came back to fetch it. She grasped it around the middle, then after a few steps she stopped, put it down to improve her grip, and carried it up to the summit and then out of Pieter's view. (The cubs were now 4 days old.) Pieter rejoined me and we waited half an hour until Penny came back to us. She was thirsty and hungry and again wanted us to come with her; when we refused to do this she was very reluctant to leave us. Since we wanted her to return to her cubs we drove home.

On the following morning she was waiting for us at the spot where we had recently taken to parking the car. Again she was very thirsty, which surprised us since the *karai* was less than a kilometer away. We had brought a dead rabbit, hoping that she would carry it to her new lair, thus showing us where it was. Instead she stood up and refused to eat the rabbit. I carried fresh water to the *karai* but found it full, so I went back to the car. Penny and Pieter were there waiting for me. They had left the rabbit halfway up the rock. When half an hour had passed we thought it high time for Penny to go back to her cubs so we coaxed her toward the rabbit, hoping that she would take it to her lair. She did nothing of the sort, and when we turned back she followed us to the car. However, next morning when we joined her we found some rabbit fur under the tree where we had parked the car the previous night, so Penny must have taken it and eaten it there, abandoning her cubs for a while longer.

Since we knew that the highest mortality among newborn cubs occurs when they are deserted by their mother while she is hunting, we hoped to reduce this risk by providing Penny with both food and water near her den, but she never seemed to be in a hurry to get back to her young and was always anxious to stay with us. Today, after her meal she again wanted us to follow her to the rock. She leaped effortlessly from boulder to boulder while Pieter performed prodigious acrobatics, wedging himself through narrow gaps, clinging to small ledges, and heaving himself from cliff to cliff. Luckily he had long legs, which helped. I watched him, through field-glasses, hoist himself inch by inch up a sheer wall of rock and felt very depressed that at the climax of my experiment, my physical disability prevented me from visiting the cubs. At least it was lucky that Penny trusted Pieter and was prepared to lead him to her nursery, for up to now there had been no record of mother/young behavior in wild leopards before the cubs were 6 months old.

When Pieter rejoined me at the foot of the hill he told me that I could not hope to reach the new lair, which was in a cave between two cliffs over which large boulders formed a roof; the opening was in a cleft so narrow that Pieter had had to wriggle through. He then saw a cave about 1 meter wide, 2 meters long, and ⅔ meter high. When the sun was in a certain position it shone in through the entrance for a short distance; the rest of the cave was dark and completely rainproof. Pieter had squatted outside it and watched the sleeping cubs until Penny began suckling them. It was by then too dark for him to take any photographs but at least he was able to reassure me that they would be safe from any predator when Penny was not there to defend the narrow opening.

Next morning we found her waiting by the parking tree. After eating and drinking, she played hide-and-seek with us; though we led her half-way up the rock three times, she seemed to have no intention of going back to the cubs. After she had deserted them for three hours Pieter scrambled up to the summit, hoping that Penny would follow him; instead, she stayed with me at the *karai*, though she followed every one of Pieter's movements with her eyes. He spent ten minutes at the mouth of the den, watching the cubs, and then began to make his way down, at which point Penny started to climb up; she and Pieter passed within 20 meters of each other, but she did not greet him. After this we drove home, hoping that once we had gone Penny would look after her family more assiduously. I thought that so long as there was no predator about she was entitled to a break and a return to her old routine; however, when I saw six birds of prey circling above the lair next day I was alarmed. Pieter struggled up to have a look; when he reached the den he found a hawk sitting on a tree so close that he was able to throw a stone at the bird, whereupon it flew off. Penny meanwhile watched him closely, but made no attempt to climb up and defend her offspring. Instead, when Pieter returned she followed us back to the car.

The cubs were now 8 days old and Pieter reported that their eyes had opened. Penny's behavior was unpredictable: next day when he followed her up to the rock, she turned around and charged him. But however unpredictable her behavior might be, so long as her teats were wet we knew the cubs had suckled and could be presumed safe.

On the following day she repeated her peculiar behavior, guiding Pieter up the rocks and then charging him. Afterwards she went off in a new direction and we assumed that she had again moved her lair. Hoping to discover where it was, we arrived next time with a rabbit. She carried it up to the far side of the outcrop, repeatedly waiting for Pieter to follow her. When he reached the ledge she suddenly attacked him, even nipping one of his fingers. He came down immediately, but strangely, she followed him, leaving the rabbit on the ledge. When they had reached the foot of the hill Penny again became most affectionate and licked his hand. It seemed as though so long as we were on the plain she was relaxed and friendly, but if Pieter followed her even for a short distance up the rock, her attitude changed. I wondered whether for the first eight days following the cubs' birth, my imprint on her had proved stronger than her instinct to defend her young but that later the situation was reversed. If so, this must have been very confusing to her, since undoubtedly she wished to preserve her affectionate relationship with me. Perhaps what she was now doing was her solution to the problem: on the plain we were all friends, but if we approached her nursery she became a wild leopardess defending her young from human predators.

Her anxiety must have increased when a lion, as well as a troop of baboons, invaded the area around Between Rock. After this we were unable to locate Penny for a day; then we saw her creeping very cautiously through the grass toward us, her belly to the ground. She kept on looking around suspiciously, and taking cover behind every tuft of grass. As I walked very slowly toward her carrying her water bowl she still kept hiding but when we met and I stroked her and tried to reassure her, she uttered that curious faint chirping which she used when worried and which certainly had some particular significance for her. After eating her calcium ration she cautiously retraced her steps. We then went back as far as Far Rock, where she sat down and blocked our way. She was listening intently and looking into a nearby thicket, which made us suppose that the cubs were quite close and that she did not wish us to see where they were.

They were now 13 days old and could certainly not have walked the 2 kilometers from Far Rock, so Penny must have carried them. We fed her meat and gave her water and, believing that she must be very tired and thirsty, decided to return during the daytime with further supplies. Now she began jumping at us and it was plain that she wanted to be left alone.

When we came back we saw her spoor along the road close to Far Rock and, examining it, it seemed to us that she must have carried the cubs in installments for another kilometer. So when we met her we were not surprised that she was both tired and thirsty. Nevertheless she led us 200 meters up the face of Far Rock and then stayed put. We reckoned that she had moved the cubs in three stages, probably to save them from baboons, and she must have made the trip during the hottest hours of the day.

Next morning we saw her high up on Far Rock, sitting near a cave. She came down to join us and, as usual, her nipples were wet. She stored the rabbit we had brought in a cleft of the rock. We set up the *karai* near her present location, hoping to prevent her from going to the river to drink.

To my dismay, I now developed what I took to be malaria, so Pieter had to go alone to look for Penny. It took him a long time to meet up with her since the baboons had followed her and were now at Far Rock, from which she had vanished. Finally he located her, well concealed in a thicket into which no baboons could follow. He realized from her behavior that the cubs were close. She walked him in a wide circle and then dismissed him, evidently intending that he should not see the cubs. By the next day the baboons had left Far Rock. We did not care for it as a location for her family as it was too close to the tourist route, but perhaps Penny had taken account of this, for she had chosen a lair as far as possible from the thicket, between sheer cliffs which even a baboon would have some difficulty in climbing. The lair was on the far side of the outcrop and provided her with a perfect observatory. Here she rested for the next few days, coming down only in the early morning to be fed and watered.

Meanwhile my supposed malaria proved to be typhoid fever, so I was obliged to spend five days in Wamba hospital from which Pieter then collected me. On our way to camp we passed Far Rock and I called to Penny. She approached, but stopped in front of me, her pupils dilated and looking as though she intended to charge. When I talked reassuringly to her she calmed down, though not before she had made one jump at me. Possibly this was because on this day I was wearing a colored blouse; usually I wore khaki shorts and a green canvas apron back and front. I had noticed similar reactions when living with Elsa and Pippa's families; apparently they recognized us by our familiar clothes rather than by our movements, appearance, or scent. Could this be because animals never change their clothes, and so do not expect human beings to do so?

Pieter now had to go to Nairobi for five days. Because of Penny's mistrust of Mrefu, I had to keep him out of her sight and carry the receiver, the big water can, and the camera myself. I did not take the heavy rifle, for I knew that Penny would never choose an area frequented by lions; but once again the baboons covered Far Rock, and during the night she had moved the cubs to a distant thicket. I traced her there and she came into the open in response to my call but looked around suspiciously, ate quickly, and went back into the thicket. On my next visit the baboons had left Far Rock, but Penny had moved to Opposite Rock; a little later I met her on the plain between the two outcrops. While she was drinking I noticed that her teats were dry, but since she behaved as though the cubs were near, I put this down to her long walk. No doubt she had had to cover the distance several times while moving the cubs one at a time.

To my surprise she now led me back to Far Rock, often stopping, listening, and winding on the way. We went to the thicket where she had hidden yesterday, and she remained there for some time while I watched six vultures flying right above the cliff where Penny had recently had her lair. She, too, saw them, moved halfway up the hill, and then stopped and stayed put. I now assumed that the cubs were at the back of Far Rock, so I collected a rabbit and gave it to Penny, thinking that she would take it back to her lair. Instead, she carried it into the thicket, and that was the last I saw of her. I was puzzled by her behavior, and next day became still more perplexed. She was near the cliff, and though she heard me call, she proceeded to move up it; when she returned, she ate only two pieces of meat instead of her usual eight and then went up the cliff by the steepest route, obviously still expecting me to follow her. As I was carrying the water can and meat bucket I was handicapped, and perhaps Penny took this into account, for several times when we came to gaps which I could not leap over she turned, came back to me, and gave me a lead by an easier way, always waiting for me until I caught up with her. Finally we came to a wall of rock; there appeared to be no way around it, and I was defeated. Penny sat herself down on a ledge just above me and waited. She kept on looking into a narrow cleft just wide enough for her to wedge herself in, and quite impossible for me to enter.

I imagined that the cubs might now be ready to eat meat, so I placed all the meat we had brought on the ledge Penny was sitting on, hoping that she would then take it back to the cubs. She grabbed two pieces and disappeared up the cliff.

CHAPTER FIFTEEN

A Cub Is Missing

IN THE MORNING we found Penny's spoor and that of only one cub leading from Far Rock to Opposite Rock. The cubs were now 27 days old
and could easily walk 2½ kilometers. So why then did only one cub
follow her? When Penny appeared she spent an hour with me, during
which time I gave her an unskinned rabbit, hoping she would teach her
young to become proper carnivores whose meat would not have to be
cut up for them. She took the rabbit and disappeared. Since she and,
presumably, one or both cubs were now near the river, and I did not
want the cubs to follow their mother if she were in need of a drink, or
worse still, if she crossed the water—I placed the full *karai* near Penny's
favorite rock, where we had fed her before the cubs were born. Next
morning she was very close to where I had left her; her teats were wet
and sticky so I knew that at least one cub must be close. As on my previous visits, I had left the car and Mrefu where she could not have seen
them, so I could not understand why she did not wish to show me the
cubs but led me in a wide circle across the plain.

Pieter returned from Nairobi that evening, which was just as well, for
next morning Penny had moved a long way off. After some difficulty, we
found her at the lower end of the gorge, close to where the hippos had
their favorite pool. She was in a playful mood, and nibbled Pieter's hand.
Then suddenly she prevented us from moving by sitting on our feet. As

there were a few thick bushes and many large rocks nearby, we assumed that the cub was hidden among them.

It was hot, and I was sitting in the shade next to Penny when suddenly she jumped up and bit my arm. I could not think what I had done to annoy her—perhaps she just wanted us to go away! We walked to the car, a distance of 1 kilometer, and when we reached it there was Penny; evidently she had followed us, taking cover all the way. What was she up to?

For the next five days she remained between Cave Rock, the cliff, and Opposite Rock, an area scattered with large rock formations, scrub, and densely covered gullies. After drinking and eating her calcium rations quickly she was lively, eager, and full of zest, enjoying to the full the opportunities afforded by the terrain for squeezing into narrow spaces between the rocks, from which she sometimes found difficulty in extricating herself. She spent her time during the next days investigating and listening, which led us to think she was seeking her cubs. She bounded over boulders, flashed down gullies and occasionally rolled over onto her back, showing her suckled nipples and asking for our caresses; but she had no intention of showing us her cubs.

One morning we saw a leopard running from Boulder Cliff toward Opposite Rock, and very soon afterwards we saw Penny, silhouetted against the sky about 400 meters away; she was watching us. She ignored my calls and remained where she was till we walked up to her. Neither hungry nor thirsty, she then lay down for a few minutes to be stroked (and allow us to note that her teats had been recently suckled), after which she walked away to the foot of the cliff, crept under a shady bush, and dozed off. We settled some 10 meters above her and waited for her to come up for her usual food and water.

We sat there in silence for a full hour; there was no wind, the countryside was perfectly quiet, and had we not seen exactly where Penny had lain down, it would have been impossible to discern any trace of a leopard in that bush, so well was she camouflaged. She continued her siesta and we moved to a nearby boulder, a favorite feeding place of hers, but we had to wait quite a while longer before she turned up. She condescended to eat a little meat, though nothing like her usual ration. Afterwards she walked off to another bush and dismissed us.

We wondered if the leopard we had seen that morning had helped to feed her and whether he had been friendly or hostile to her cubs. Before she had conceived, Penny had always evaded us when a leopard was near, but now that she had her family what role did a male play in her life?

Next morning we could get no signal though Pieter climbed several high rocks to cover a wide area. It occurred to me that Penny might be in the gorge; if she were in one of its caves it would be possible to get a signal only if the receiver were directly opposite the mouth of her hiding place. So Pieter walked along the bottom of the gorge with the receiver while I waited with meat and water at the top and Mrefu and the car stayed at a safe distance with the supplementary rations.

An hour passed and a long hour it seemed. What if Pieter had hurt himself or met lions? I was consoling myself that we had seen no lion spoors nor heard vervets, who always sounded the alarm at the approach of a predator, when at last he appeared, walking very slowly, with Penny behind him.

He had searched the gorge right down to the end where the hippo pool was, investigating every possible hideout on the way, but he received no sign or signal. While down by the pool he looked up and there, on the cliff immediately above him, was Penny with a cub gamboling around her. It looked in excellent condition, and as soon as he called her, both of them tumbled down the rocks to a sand bank immediately opposite to where he was standing. This was about half a kilometer from the natural bridge where Penny always crossed; he had a perfect view of the cub playing with its mother but when it tried to bite her leg she sent it flying and both disappeared in the direction of the boulder bridge. Later Penny crossed over without the cub, and followed Pieter up the gorge. Finally she flung herself down, exhausted, at my feet while I noted with satisfaction that she was still being suckled. But where was the other cub? Had it fallen victim to a predator?

While Penny was eating, we planned how to reunite her with her cub; this, we hoped, would afford us the opportunity to give it meat.

Pippa's offspring had started eating meat five weeks to the day after their birth. Penny's cubs were now 36 days old, and having been told that leopards develop quicker than any other cats, I thought her cub might have been needing meat for several days. I had never seen her regurgitating though I hoped that the rabbits we provided had been shared.

Pieter decided to return with Penny to the platform overlooking the natural bridge while I would collect a rabbit from the car and meet them there, hoping that Penny might either bring the cub across to us or else take the rabbit back with her and feed it to him where we could see it. We met at the rendezvous, but all that happened was that Penny took the rabbit away, in a different direction from the one we had expected, and hid it in a gully. She then followed us back almost to the car, a distance of about a kilometer, where we fed her the rest of the chopped-up meat and left. We were concerned that for several days now Pieter had only seen one cub. Why had Penny come over the river alone? Had she followed the leopard we had seen yesterday—and possibly left a cub with him? This didn't seem likely.

Next morning when she appeared we had the assurance that she was still suckling at least one cub for her nipples were sticky. She hardly moved all morning and ate very little. Pieter went back to the car for another rabbit while I rested with Penny under a shady rock, stroking her, to which she responded most affectionately. Suddenly she sat up, looked at me with half-closed eyes, and before I could stop her, she bit me in the stomach through the canvas apron. What could be going on in her head? Would I ever learn to anticipate her reactions? For a long time she had been so gentle; yet she had bitten me twice during the last few days for no reason that I could guess. Afterwards she sneaked away to hide under a bush as if she knew that she was in disgrace.

Our routine during recent weeks was to locate Penny, then leave the car with Mrefu a long way behind and walk in silence toward her so that if the cub were with her we would not frighten it away. These tactics worked to some extent: we managed to meet without having to call her, but she never showed us her cub.

One day she led us in a most determined way, without a single stop, right across the open plain between the cliff and Opposite Rock. She had never done this before, for she always made a point of avoiding crossing open ground. When we came to the base of Opposite Rock we heard stones falling from halfway up and spotted a hyena scrambling to the summit. Penny rushed a short way up the rocks, then sat down and would not budge. It was still early for her meal but when we offered it to her she gobbled it up quickly as though she wanted to be rid of us. We were as eager as she seemed to be to discover whether the hyena had harmed her cub, so we left at once.

For the first few days or weeks of its life, every animal is unconscious of its genus; it only eats, digests, and sleeps. This is the period when, should the infant be adopted by a human being, that person will become permanently imprinted on the creature and will be given all the trust and affection that it would normally share only with its natural family. As development continues, however, it is as though there comes a point when the genus of the animal is established, after which it is impossible to reach the rapport which very early association between differing species can achieve. This development occurs at varying speeds in different species: a dog's identity is established in nineteen days but with a lion it takes six weeks. Elsa was 3 weeks old when we adopted her, and I was closer to her than to any other animal I have had, but even she concealed her cubs from me for the first weeks of their life. In their case, had I so wished, I could probably have made them tame, though only with the help of their mother, but of course what I wanted for them was that they should be brought up absolutely wild. To this end, I never touched them though it was sometimes very hard to resist the temptation to do so.

I was not worried that Penny would now hide her remaining cub from us though at first she had wanted us to see it. I felt she would know instinctively the right time for us to meet. It was now thirty-nine days since she had given birth. We were full of hope when Penny met us and took us as fast as she could across the open plain to the base of the cliff. We settled close to several large rocks which formed caves and crevices, with shady trees which hid their entrances. It seemed to us a perfect area for a nursery. Penny lay down in a bush and licked her paws, staring at the rocks and listening intently. We stood about 3 meters off, motionless and silent. After a short while Penny leaped up, made her way to a cave, and disappeared into it. We expected the cub to appear at any moment.

But after ten minutes she returned alone, came down the rocks, laid her head on her paws, and dozed off. A single baboon began to bark from Opposite Rock but she barely raised her head even when he repeated his performance. Now and again she gazed at the rocks. Since she was suckling her cub and had been guarding this area for the last two hours, we thought it must be close by. I was determined that, exasperating and exhausting as our vigil would undoubtedly be, I would stick it out.

As the minutes and hours passed, Penny seemed to feel our departure was overdue. For about two and a half hours we stayed put; then Penny got up lazily, stretched herself, and suddenly leaped across the 3 meters which separated us and jumped at us—her usual mode of dismissal. We not only stood our ground but offered her water, which she drank. Her failure to drive us away by force seemed to disconcert her and she loitered around indecisively for ten minutes as if not knowing what to do. Then she walked slowly off across the plain toward Opposite Rock. Halfway there she rested under a shady tree and again tried to jump us off but we stopped this with a firm "No!" so she continued her circuitous journey to the base of Opposite Rock, where she flopped down. By now it was midday and high time for her to return to her cub, wherever it was, so I decided to admit defeat and leave her to her own devices. Penny had again succeeded in keeping her cub concealed.

Ten kilometers from camp, our car track led first along the cliff facing the thicket and then turned at a sharp bend. Here begins what we named the Loop because the track runs first along the base of the other side of the cliff, facing Opposite Rock, until it almost reaches the Boulder, Penny's favorite feeding place; from there it turns in a half circle to the base of Opposite Rock and continues along it until this outcrop ends in a gentle, rocky slope which we named Lion Rock after watching two prides on it. Here the Loop ends as the track divides, one fork leading straight on to Far Rock, about 2 kilometers away, the other turning sharply to the right around Lion Rock and leading to the river. For the first 500 meters it keeps close to the base of Opposite Rock, then turns at a right angle to the river some 500 meters downhill. Leaving the track at this last bend and walking along the base of Far Rock for about 300 meters, one reaches the other end of Opposite Rock which here falls in sheer cliffs into the river, forming the beginning of Penny's Gorge. From there one can only reach the natural bridge half a kilometer downstream by scrambling across these cliffs.

Penny appeared to have selected her next den high up on Opposite Rock, facing the river near Lion Rock, for she always came down from that area as soon as she heard our car. Indeed, for the next three days she was unwilling to let these rocks out of her sight, no doubt to keep an eye on two ravens which hovered overhead from time to time. But here she was very close to the river and the natural bridge, so we once more placed the *karai* near her rocks, hoping to make it unnecessary for her to go to the river for a drink or, worse still, cross it with her cub. One of my anxieties, that of Penny's meat supply, seemed to be temporarily in abeyance, for near the lair we supposed her to be occupying, the rocks were covered with so many white patches it looked as though they must have been whitewashed. This was the dried urine of hyrax. The rock-hyrax is a small diurnal animal which sleeps during the night in rocky crevices; Penny, who was nocturnal, would have excellent opportunities to catch them. We observed that she was putting on weight rapidly and felt sure that she was not only eating the meat we took to her but supplementing her diet during the night.

Opposite Rock was often occupied by baboons, and we were worried when we saw a large troop sitting above Lion Rock obviously watching something. As we drew near, we saw a girl dressed in a bright red loincloth and blouse sitting high up on Lion Rock. I went up and asked her if she had permission to walk around here alone and I told her that earlier that day we had watched five lion cubs huddled together near the track—

obviously having been ordered by their mothers to stay put till they returned from hunting. We knew this pride, which only a few days ago had
been near our camp.

The girl said she was with a party camping near the river, and that
only that morning they had been attacked by baboons who had carried
off clothing, cameras, passports, travelers' checks, and other possessions.
She had been looking for them and had found some of their missing
equipment on the rock. I was sorry about the baboons but I explained
that I should nevertheless have to report her. I asked her to come with
me to the car and told her I would drive back to her camp and get her
address. It was strictly against the Park rules to walk alone so far from a
car or a camp and it was in everybody's interest that these rules be kept.
We drove around Lion Rock and met five more of her party, all dressed
in similarly unsuitable clothes. They were watching Penny, who was hiding among the rocks. Quickly I ushered all of them into the car; and
leaving Pieter and Mrefu to cope with Penny, I drove to their camp,
which was about a kilometer from Lion Rock.

There I met the rest of the party, twelve in all. Judging by the two
small mountain tents, each of which would only hold two people, by the
many foam-rubber sheets, and the sleeping bags around, most of these
people must have slept on the ground in the open within a few meters of
the riverbush which offered splendid cover for any wild animal. The
baboons had obviously taken this chance to play with such tempting toys
and had made off with as many as they could carry. Most of the important items had now been recovered—but when the campers had discovered their loss, instead of going to one of the entrance gates to report
the baboon invasion and ask for an armed escort to accompany them in
their search, they had wandered about on their own. I pointed out that
they had violated the camping rules by sleeping in the open, on the
ground, in a park where predators could have endangered them. They
replied that they did not know the rules, to which I could only answer
that ignorance of a rule is no excuse for breaking it. I took down all their
addresses. This was not popular, but I had to act as I did because such
irresponsible behavior endangered not only themselves but also the animals for whom they provided much temptation.

The Elsa Wild Animal Appeal had just completed a three-year research project on the impact tourism has on national parks, and only a
few weeks ago had again been asked to finance research on the ways in
which cheetahs particularly suffer through being constantly surrounded
by cars and people filming them. This either leads to their killing their

cubs, or to their leaving the Park. Unfortunately, drivers are often bribed by clients to help them get good pictures; often, too, they have little authority and cannot prevent deplorable behavior such as throwing stones at elephants to stir them into action. Pamphlets instructing visitors how to behave in a game park were issued at the gates, but these were as a rule a waste of money. The only way to catch offenders red-handed would be to have honorary Game Wardens in civilian clothes patrol in private cars, because the uniforms of patroling Rangers gave the offenders ample warning. But to work this plan needed far more money than was available, and as a result many wild animals were so harassed that they stopped breeding.

When I got back to Penny after this incident, I found her in a highly nervous state; though Pieter and I tried to reassure her, she soon disappeared into the rocks. By next morning she had calmed down and was once more very affectionate. It may have been due to the calcium lactate we gave her that she was always heavy in milk; indeed, I believe she could have nursed a baby elephant. Two of her teats had been recently suckled, and she was so friendly that she allowed us to follow her some 50 meters into the rocks. On our way we rested and fed her several times to assure her that we did not want to spy on her cub or go farther than she wished us to. We believed that she must have found a secure cave for her nursery, as she ignored the barking of a baboon and, settling for a snooze, watched our departure.

Next day, to our consternation, we got a signal from the river near the natural bridge, but my calls evidently diverted Penny from crossing to the far side, for she soon joined us at the beginning of the gorge. She was in a very odd state, growling and swaying and rolling about and rubbing herself against us. She did not want us to touch her, and did not eat her meat; she lay down for a rest, only to start up and begin the whole performance again. All her teats were dry. She followed us back to her rocks, though very slowly, and on the way repeated these strange submission rites. Bit by bit she ate her meat ration and then moved out of sight.

Worried about the cub, we returned at tea time to try to find out if she was with it. Penny scrambled down to greet us and we were reassured to find three of her teats had been freshly suckled. She still made her submission rites though she seemed more relaxed and, after a short walk, led us up the rocks to where we had left her in the morning. To make sure that the cub would not starve, we had brought a rabbit. Grabbing it, she looked around for a place to store it and eventually chose a bush in the opposite direction from where we imagined her den to be; after this she followed us half a kilometer to the car, and watched us drive away.

Our surprise visit to Penny that afternoon had relieved our anxiety about the cub but we were baffled by her behavior. If she were now in oestrus for the first time after her accouchement, why was she showing submission symptoms and searching for a male? Neither Elsa nor Pippa had shown an interest in a male while they were nursing their young, and I expected Penny to behave in the same way.

We were even more bewildered when next morning we received Penny's signal from 500 meters across the river. As soon as I called her I saw her emerging from behind a bush—she was alone. She walked very slowly toward us, often looking back over her shoulder until she reached the river bank opposite us. She stood there for a few minutes, looking first at us and then back to the bush; finally she walked off downstream and out of sight. Meanwhile, I raked the plain through the binoculars but did not see the cub or a male.

Fifteen minutes later Penny joined us; since she was dry she must have crossed by the natural bridge about half a kilometer away. She had not been suckled recently, we saw no spoor of the cub, and she was showing even stronger submission symptoms than yesterday. Growling and rolling around, she followed us back to the rocks where we supposed her den to be and ended up where she had hidden the rabbit. We found it untouched except for a small wound below its throat. We did not stay long, so that she would go back as soon as possible to her cub. In the afternoon when we returned, Penny came down from the same place and we saw that three of her teats were sticky; this was reassuring. After a slow, short walk we all rested in the rocks near the rejected rabbit. Fondling her, and watching her squeezing herself between the rocks in a desperate effort to find some surface other than ourselves on which to rub herself, I wondered what urges drove her to behave like this. She seemed to me to be torn between three incompatible forces: her maternal instinct, her sexual impulse, and her relationship with us. Which would prove the strongest?

CHAPTER SIXTEEN

Happy Ending

FOR THE NEXT four days we got no signal from Penny, but there were fresh spoors of a male leopard leading from close to Opposite Rock to the river and back again. So far as we could judge, he had not crossed to the other side. This made us believe that Penny was not far away; for one thing she was clearly seeking a male, and for another she needed to be near the river since she was always thirsty.

There was a large lugga 10 kilometers upstream which ran down to the river and contained three deep caves. We searched them, but in vain, after which we drove 20 kilometers downstream to Borji Hill, the highest point for miles around. Pieter and Makedde struggled up the steep lava slope from the top of which they could overlook the whole area, but saw no sign of Penny. Every morning we went up Turkana Hill, from which we had a wide view, but with no success. We could not imagine that she had taken her cub far from the river and into the waterless hinterland, or that she was a long way away from the male. Since the arrival of the cubs we had never before been so long without getting a signal, and I was tormented by the idea that Penny had been taken by a crocodile and that the surviving cub was starving.

After yet another sleepless night, I decided to follow the fresh male spoors, hoping they would lead us to Penny. It was a Sunday, and we had to start early so as to be ahead of the tourist traffic which would spoil his spoors on the tracks. We made straight for the Loop and then prepared to search the far side of the river, should we fail to find Penny nearer home.

Suddenly we received from very close a signal right above us on Opposite Rock; then, seconds later, I saw Penny coming out from behind a boulder. We were walking along the Loop, and she looked down at us for a few minutes and then disappeared behind a patch of sansevieria.

The signal then stopped, so we knew she must have moved over the summit to the side facing the river. We drove around quickly and there she was, scrambling down the rocks to meet us. She was very thirsty and hungry, and had lost weight. We saw that two of her teats had been freshly suckled, and her vulva was covered with dried blood which she licked frequently. Had she mated? Would she conceive again so soon after giving birth?

As soon as she had finished the last scrap of meat, she led us determinedly up the rocks and, as she had done on the day the cubs were newly born, she waited for me to catch up with her when I got left behind. Pieter helped me, and at last we reached the cave where we thought she was living. But now she evidently had a different nursery. At this point I felt defeated and could go no further. Together Pieter and Penny disappeared and I sat down to wait, feeling bitterly disappointed. After what seemed a very long half hour, I saw Pieter running along the track around Lion Rock toward the car. Fearing that he was in danger, I struggled down as quickly as I could. He greeted me with the marvelous news that Penny had led him to the place on Opposite Rock where he had got her signal earlier that morning and where there were two large boulders forming a rainproof tunnel. She disappeared into it. Next he saw her carrying her cub by the neck around a rock and out of sight. When she came back to the tunnel alone, Pieter followed her to the entrance. After a few minutes she went to collect the cub. Carrying it by the neck she passed within a few inches of Pieter and dropped it. It ran into the tunnel but she brought it back and suckled it near him; then she licked it tenderly till it started playing with her, pulling her ears. Suddenly it saw Pieter and darted at once deep into the tunnel. Penny called it back with a low moan; it came, and she licked it all over till it suckled her again.

Pieter said the cub's eyes were very large, and still brown; it was now 51 days old and the size of a small cat. It was in excellent condition, fat even, still gray, and beautifully marked. Pieter left Penny still suckling and hurried down to bring me the news—it was a splendid ending to the last four days of anxiety.

We did not want to alarm Penny by driving back, as she might mistake the noise of our car for that of a stranger, so we arranged that Makedde should search for spoors of the male while Pieter walked back a little way with me and then climbed up to Penny to take photographs. Meanwhile I would walk on back to the Loop, watching Pieter through field-glasses and hoping to see where Penny's new lair was.

The role played by the male in Penny's present life remained a mystery. Was he providing prey for his family as well as satisfying their mother's sexual demands? Even if the male helped Penny, she needed feeding, so Pieter and I returned at tea time with meat and a rabbit. We found her resting near the entrance to her tunnel, watching us calmly. While she came slowly down to us we installed the *karai* between the rocks, hidden from the track. She had a long drink from it and ate some more meat but would not go for a walk with us. So we rested together, she licking our hands while we stroked her and searched for ticks.

When we gave her the rabbit she quickly carried it higher up and hid it and soon afterwards she went back to her den. We saw her bring out not one but two cubs, settle with them on a rock, and then lie down beside them. While they cuddled between her forelegs and patted her face with their paws she looked down at us with an expression of proud fulfillment and immense happiness which she wanted to share with us. I had been overjoyed that morning to know that she had one living cub. Now my happiness was complete, since I knew that in spite of the dangers of lions, baboons, and tourists, Penny had succeeded in rearing both her cubs for fifty-one days. She would no longer be alone.

At last I had a perfect view of the family, even though the lenses of my field-glasses were a little misty.

POSTSCRIPT

*This book stops at the point at which Joy Adamson intended the first
volume of her leopard experiment to end. Had she lived, she would have
followed the lives of Penny's descendants as she had those of Elsa and
Pippa, and there would have been a second volume. This is lost to us, but
since we believe that Joy's readers and friends would like to know something about the last months of her life, we are reproducing in this section
her account of certain events which took place in this fraught period. The
most distressing and dramatic was a fire at her camp. It had been preceded by a terrible drought.*

THERE WAS STILL another six weeks to wait till the long rains would
start. The short rains had failed north of the Equator and Shaba had
become a dust bowl in which only animals used to desert conditions could
survive, and those had all congregated near the river.

One day we surprised some two thousand head of cattle at a swamp
inside the boundary. This was the home of the local buffalo and of the
few elephants which had survived the years of poaching. With the increasing drought the far side of the river, the forbidden military zone,
became dotted with livestock whose bellowing was accompanied by a
chopping sound as trees were felled to make night enclosures for the
herdsmen. Soon the barren plain became even more denuded, and sand-
devils of alarming height whirled across the area. . . .

We were having trouble with our two refrigerators. Indeed, recently
one of them had nearly exploded in Pieter's face. So on September 15
we sent for an expert to examine them. Having made a thorough checkup,
he assured us that they seemed to be in good order. That afternoon Pieter

drove him back to Isiolo, and since it was a Sunday our staff accompanied them.

Alone in the camp, I started to clean up the dining tent, where the work on the refrigerators had taken place. Suddenly there was an explosion. Flame burst from one of the machines and set fire to the canvas of the tent. I tried to put it out with a broom and a duster, but the heat was so intense that I soon had to rush into the open. Standing there I watched the flames shoot up into the trees and ignite the thatched roof of our living hut, which in a matter of seconds became an inferno. Panic-stricken, I stupidly dashed inside and grabbed the tape recorder. Nearly suffocated by the flames, I came out very rapidly. As though paralyzed I stood watching the raging hell around me. Had I not been rooted to the spot, I might have been able to release the rabbits; my failure to do so haunted me for weeks to come.

Blown at great speed by a strong wind the flames crossed the camp and approached the nearby bushes and the plain beyond. As soon as I recovered my wits, I seized a hessian bag and beat the flames as they neared the bushes. If they caught fire, I would be trapped.

As I passed the rabbits' boma I recognized the calcinated remains of my favorite among them. She had died protecting her four young with her body. The sight appalled me, for I felt that perhaps I might have saved them; but this was no time for remorse. The crackling and the infernal heat urged me to action. I went on beating the flames, though I had difficulty in breathing and my skin was scorched. My one aim now was to prevent the fire from reaching the bush behind the camp. Already the shoulder-high reeds by the swamp were smoldering, and beyond them a purple column rose skyward surrounded by pitch-black smoke. The spectacle was horrifying. Later I learned that the purple smoke was due to some tear-gas canisters that had been buried in Shaba at the time of the Mau Mau troubles.

At six in the evening three Rangers from the Shaba Gate Post, having seen the smoke, walked in. It was an immense relief no longer to be alone. As we extinguished the embers in what had been our camp I began to take in the extent of the loss the fire had caused us; our radio, by which we could communicate with the outside, Penny's telemetric receiver, our furniture, crockery, cutlery, lamps, books, the Bolex movie camera, and all our food were gone. Worse still, my photographic records of Penny, except for the collection I had providentially sent to London to illustrate my book, had been destroyed. Now these were the only survivors of 4,500 stills and a similar footage of movie film. The only objects that had survived the fire were my little Omega watch, still ticking beneath the ashes, and the pelvic bones and shoulder blades of the elephants we had collected and lined up against the fences as a grim reminder of the heavy poaching of the past and as a challenge to us to restore the natural fauna to Shaba. The gruesome collection stood glaringly white amid the ashes.

When Pieter returned, he told me that the smoke from the camp had been visible 65 kilometers away in Isiolo. The Rangers who had arrived earlier now asked Pieter to drive them to the Park Gate 22 kilometers away. From there they could report the fire to the Samburu Warden and ask for beaters to prevent the flames from spreading. After they had left, I sat on a tin trunk that had contained our provisions, which were boiled to pulp. I looked into the darkness and saw the skeletons of the dead trees glowing red against the black velvet of the sky. The scene was beautiful but I could not enjoy it, for these glowing trunks were the sentinels surrounding a tragedy in which countless small creatures had died. At midnight the men returned disconsolate. At the Park Gate the radio was out of order and the Warden was on safari.

Very early next morning we all drove to Isiolo to report the fire. To my great relief, the Councilors were very sympathetic and dispatched a truck full of beaters to help us. The engineer who had attended to the refrigerator that had exploded was terribly upset and inclined to blame himself, but I was able to reassure him that it was almost certainly not his fault; I had heard of several refrigerators of the same make that had exploded. He promised to send a builder friend the next day to help set up a new camp. Having collected a few essentials, we started back and were much reassured when we met the beaters and they told us that a flow of lava had acted as a natural firebreak.

On our way home we had searched, without success, for Penny, but at least we knew that the fire had never reached her territory. In spite of this, coming home was grim. The wind was still strong, and ash-devils were dancing across the plain. We hung our provisions out of reach of rats and ants and made our supper by the flickering light of a kerosene lamp while discussing plans for our new home. Meanwhile, we had been lucky enough to find a Turkana who was prepared to help us tidy up the debris. In the morning we again searched for Penny, and found her. She was very glad to see us.

After two days the workmen arrived, five men, some of whom had never been in the bush before and were excited at the prospect of seeing wild animals. Indeed, when a lion whuffed close by, I was only just in time to prevent one of the men from walking into the thicket from which the sounds came, to have a close look at a lion. It was essential that the rebuilding work should be done quickly, for the rains were due soon, and when they came, the roads would be flooded and the potholes invisible. Come they did, and even the four-wheel-drive Toyota got stuck and the Peugeot became quite useless.

One day, when we were on our way to the tented camp, from which we hoped to radio-call my friend Peter Johnson and ask him to buy us two refrigerators, the car got stuck up to its hubcaps. Pieter walked to the Shaba Gate to get some Rangers to come to our aid; I remained on guard in the car. Unfortunately, the rescue party also got stuck, so by the time Pieter and the three men arrived it was almost sunset. All four crawled under our car in an effort to raise it, but did not succeed. Finally, Pieter and I decided to walk home, escorted by an armed Ranger in case we met lions. It was a moonless night. Walking over the lava and the pebbles was by no means easy, and after we had gone 5 kilometers I fell and hurt my knee badly. Over the next 5 kilometers Pieter supported me both physically and morally; indeed, without his help I do not think I could have made it.

Next day we drove to Wamba hospital, where an X-ray showed that I had a bad crack. So again I was put in a plaster cast, which prevented me from driving and made walking difficult. Nor was this our only trouble. My good old friend the cook, Kifosha, left us, and it was very difficult to find anyone willing to take a post in a remote camp where the only entertainment was an occasional fishing expedition. The new camp progressed slowly, but in the end it was completed and we moved in thankfully. . . .

Not long afterwards there was a mysterious burglary. I had given Pieter 1,028 shillings to cover our weekly shopping. He put the money into a little cabinet in his tent which had no lock. He then went out for a very short time, and when he returned found the money had gone. We called the police, who searched the camp but with no result. This was not surprising, since there had been plenty of time to hide the money in a hole in the ground before the police arrived.

A little later, when Pieter and the staff had gone to Isiolo to shop, I experienced "a gentle but effective warning." On my early-morning stroll near the camp I suddenly heard what I took to be an aircraft rather close and stood still to listen to it. Then suddenly I realized that the noise was that of a lion growling, and I saw his head rise above the bush nearly 15 meters from me. Facing the lion, I tiptoed backward until I had put another 15 meters between us. Then I turned and walked home quickly.

Next day on our walk to Penny we passed the lion at the same place. He was chewing a kill. I recognized him as an old friend, a young male who had often been near the camp and was always alone.

On Thursday, January 3, 1980, Joy Adamson went out for her customary evening stroll. She usually returned in time to hear the evening news on the radio. When she failed to appear, a search was made, and her body was found a hundred meters outside the camp enclosure.

The dead are not under the earth
They are in the tree that rustles
They are in the woods that groan
They are in the water that runs
They are in the water that sleeps
They are in the hut, they are in the crowd
The dead are not dead.
Those who are dead are never gone
They are in the breast of a woman
They are in the child that is wailing
 and in the fire that flames.
The dead are not under the earth
They are in the fire that is dying
They are in the grass that is weeping
They are in the whimpering rocks
They are in the forest, they are in the house
They are not dead.

When my ancestors talk about the Creator they say:
He is with us . . . We sleep with him. We hunt with him.
We dance with him.

FRANCIS NNAGGENDA

APPENDICES

❖

Leopard Habits

BIRTH: Penny wanted to show us her two cubs a few hours after they were born. We followed her on the third day. She showed us the cubs for one week, until they opened their eyes, then kept hiding them off and on.

MOVING CUBS: After 4 days, from natal den. Then changed dens every 2–4 days.

STOP DRINKING MILK: 3 months.

EATING HABITS: Never hold meat with front paws, like cheetahs.

COVER FOOD WITH EARTH: Yes.

COVER EXCREMENT WITH EARTH: Yes.

EATING GRASS: Yes.

SOUND: Rasping, short cough when calling cubs, deep growl when submitting. High pitched chirp, when worried. The 3-day-old cubs made a low MMMMMM MMMMM (humming) when struggling to the teats.

FOOD-STORING INSTINCT: First taking meat up to platforms when 5½ months old.

HUNTING INSTINCT: First chased a dik-dik when 11 months.

DISGUISING OWN SCENT: By rolling in strong-scented plants when 7½ months old, later rolling in buffalo pats, elephant, hippo, and antelope droppings.

COME INTO SEASON BEFORE READY TO MATE: At 21 months.

MATING STARTS: 2 years and 2 months. Penny conceived at 26 months but had a miscarriage at 29 months. Conceived 1 month later, February 23, 1979. Gave birth to two cubs May 26, 1979.

FIRST KILL: Bala, at 9 months—rabbit.

PREY: Hares, dik-dik, francoline and other birds, rock-hyrax, mongoose, lizards.

OESTRUS: Irregular.

SOCIAL INSTINCT: Solitary—except when rearing cubs.

SCENT-MARKING TERRITORY: First at 8 months, "jetting" bushes with urine.

FINAL NECKBITE OF MALE TO FEMALE AFTER MATING: Penny was bitten when 22 months old—though had not conceived.

COMMUNICATIONS: Facial expression: hard, pin-sized pupils, eyes half closed—danger. Dilated pupils—excitement. Flattened ears—danger. Tail movements. Marking territory. Sound. Tactile.

❖

Leopard Development and Behavior

TEMPERATURE	100–102° Fahrenheit	
GESTATION	93 days	
EYES OPEN	8th day	

DECIDUOUS TEETH   Penny: if born September 1, 1976   MONTHS

Top

Jan.	10, 1977	lost 2 incisors	4⅓
	29	lost a few more	5
March 17		2 large premolars, little tips visible	6½
		2 canine	6½
May	31	right canine fell out	9
June	1	left canine fell out	9

Bottom

Jan.	10	1 incisor lost	4⅓
	29	few incisors lost	5
March 28		2 canines out, right is broken	7
		4 premolars out	7
May	22	lost left canine	8¾
	29	lost right broken canine	9
June	29	lost right premolar	10
July	11	lost left premolar	10⅓

PERMANENT TEETH

Top

March 17		4 incisors out, 1 coming through	6½
	28	5 incisors out	7
April	7	premolar tip visible	7¼
	20	all 6 incisors out	7¾
	22	right canine visible	7¾
	24	left canine visible	7¾
May	5	premolar tip through	8¼

Bottom

March 17		5 incisors out	6½
	28	all 6 incisors out	7
April	4	right canine tip visible (behind broken milk canine)	7
	7	left canine tip visible	7¼
		both molars visible	7¼
July	20	right and left premolars come out	10¾

PERMANENT TEETH,

Aug.   21, 1977

	I	C	PM	M
Top	3	1	1	2
Bottom	3	1	1	1

TEATS	4
MARKINGS	10 double rosettes from tail-rout to shoulder (Bala and Penny's son Pasha also have ten, the other cub none)
BABY FLUFF	Lost it at 4 months

❖

Penny's Measurements

	AT 1 YEAR	AT 3 YEARS
Tip of nose to back of skull	25 cm	
Back of skull to base of tail	99 cm	
Tail	69 cm	
Total length	193 cm	198 cm
	(6'4")	(6'6")
Heart girth	72 cm	
Permanent left upper canine	25 mm	
Permanent left lower canine	21 mm	
Weight	35½ kg	
	(78 lbs.)	

❖

Bala's Measurements

	AT HIS ARRIVAL, MAY 2, 1979		5 MONTHS LATER, BEFORE HIS RELEASE OCTOBER 6, 1979
Tip of nose to back of skull	22 cm		25 cm
Back of skull to base of tail	78 cm		88 cm
Tail	64 cm		72 cm
Total length	164 cm		185 cm
	(5'5")		(6'1")
Heart girth	51 cm		57 cm
Neck	34 cm		37 cm
Deciduous left upper canine (broken)	6 mm	Permanent left upper canine	19 mm
Deciduous left lower canine (broken)	0 mm	Permanent left lower canine	22 mm
Deciduous right upper canine	12 mm	Permanent right upper canine	22 mm
Deciduous right lower canine	12 mm	Permanent right lower canine	17 mm
Weight	12 kg (26 lbs.)	Weight with empty stomach after 3 days starving	26.8 kg (59 lbs.)

❖
Illnesses

PROPHYLACTIC: Penny was vaccinated against feline enteritis on 10/29/76, 11/13/76, and January 1977. Again on 8/31/77. Felidovac.

HOOKWORM: Cannex 6 tablets one day. Repeat after 2–3 weeks.

COCCIDIOSIS (Parasite): 8 tablets Trinamide first day, followed by 4 tablets daily for 4 days. If all goes well, repeat this dosage for a further 5 days after a 4-day break. Symptoms: Vomiting, diarrhoea with blood, cramps.

HEMOBARTONELLA INFECTION (red blood cell parasite): Symptoms: Pallor (pale membranes), possible loss of appetite. Treatment: long course of tetracycline 30 days—500 mg twice daily (2 capsules twice daily).

❖
Sedation

USED BY PATRICK HAMILTON, AT BALA'S ARRIVAL: 0.4 mg of CI = 744 (80 mg).

USED BY DR. PAUL SAYER BEFORE RELEASE: Ketamine 5 mg per lb together with Xylazine (Rompun) 1 mg per lb topped up with a further 100 mg Ketamine after half an hour and a further 50 mg Ketamine an hour after darting. In addition he was given penicillin and a highly potent Vitamin B & C mixture to counteract any stress effects (Parentrovite HP).

❖
General Comparison of Lions, Cheetahs, Leopards Based on Elsa, Pippa, Penny, and Their Cubs

	LIONS	CHEETAHS	LEOPARDS
CHARACTER	Being gregarious, they share their lives with each other and are easy to understand. They are very affectionate and, knowing that they have no enemy except Man, show no fear of other animals and are usually relaxed.	Being solitary, they are far more introvert than the extrovert lions, and more difficult to understand. Cheetahs know their vulnerability to lions, leopards, hyenas, and baboons and are always on the alert. They are masters in concealing themselves, which is their main defense. Their famous speed of 70 km.p.h. can only be used for some 400 meters; then they slow down.	Being solitary, nocturnal, light in weight, excellent rock and tree climbers, extremely fast in mental and physical reactions, leopards combine all the advantages any predator can have. Penny's greatest danger is baboons when outnumbering her. Lions and leopards kill each other's cubs, but avoid each other when adult. Leopard camouflage is so perfect among rocks and trees that one can only detect them by their always moving tails.

	LIONS	CHEETAHS	LEOPARDS
HABITAT (TRANSLOCATION)	Elsa, being a desert lioness (*Felix somaliense*), almost died when we translocated her from 1,000-m Isiolo to 3,000-m Mara Reserve, where *Felix masaica* live. She recovered within 2–3 weeks after we took her to Meru Nat. Park, at 1,000 m. Lions seem not to adapt well to climatic changes.	It took Pippa about 3 months to adapt herself from the cool climate of Nairobi and Naro-Moru at 2,150 m to Meru at 1,000 m, though she was never ill during that period.	Though Penny was born and reared at 1,900 m for one year, a true forest leopard, she adapted herself within 2–3 weeks to the arid Shaba country at 1,000 m, with lava, thorns, and rocky environment.
TERRITORY	Elsa's territory was about 250 square kilometers in Meru.	Pippa's territory was 165 square kilometers in Meru, which she finally allocated in sections to each litter, who never trespassed into the adjacent section of the other litter.	Penny covers a home range of 300 square kilometers, and her territory is about 140 square kilometers.
CUBS	Elsa had been orphaned when about 3 weeks old and had no mother to teach her lion behavior. She was an excellent mother to her three cubs. Lionesses put the whole head of a cub into their mouth when carrying it. Elsa, having been closest to me (I was more strongly imprinted on her than on Pippa or Penny) concealed her cubs for six weeks from us, but then made our camp the H.Q. for her family.	Pippa was found abandoned when about 3 weeks old. She, too, was a perfect mother to her four litters. Cheetahs carry their cub by the scruff of its neck. Pippa always guided me to her cubs in the bush, when the first litter was 10 days, second litter 5 days, third litter 8 days, fourth litter 10 days old. Afterwards I always had to visit the cheetahs in the bush. Only when the cubs were more than one year old did they occasionally come to camp for short visits.	Penny was found abandoned when 1 month old and had no mother to teach her except me. She, too, is a perfect mother, rearing two cubs while lion and baboon invade her area. She led us to her cubs when they were 3 days old, and during one more week. Since then she hides them, though on a few occasions took us to their dens. She had wanted to show us her cubs within a few hours of birth. After they opened their eyes at 8 days, she never brought the cubs near us, though she allowed Pieter to come near the dens high up on the rocks. The older the cubs grew, the more they kept away from us, even when Penny tried to bring us together.

	LIONS	CHEETAHS	LEOPARDS
RELATIONSHIP TO JOY	I never had any fear when being with Elsa. Even when she was ill and irritable, I could always rely on her trust and affection.	I was never afraid of Pippa, who was always relaxed and reliable with me.	Leopards are certainly the most difficult to understand, more intelligent than lions or cheetahs and less reliable. Although Penny was very good-natured, trusting, affectionate, and coopera- tive I could never relax with her.

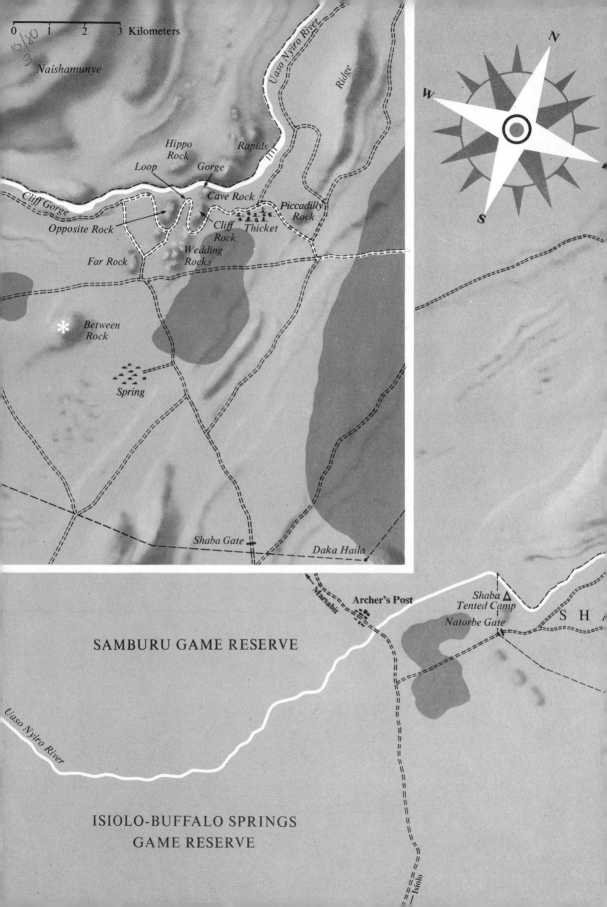

0 1 2 3 Kilometers

Naishamunye

Uaso Nyiro River

Ridge

Hippo Rock *Rapids*

Loop *Gorge*

Cliff Gorge *Cave Rock*

Opposite Rock *Piccadilly Rock*

Cliff Rock *Thicket*

Far Rock *Wedding Rocks*

Between Rock

Spring

Shaba Gate *Daka Haila*

N

W

S

Marsabit

Archer's Post

Shaba Tented Camp

Natorbe Gate

S H A

SAMBURU GAME RESERVE

Uaso Nyiro River

ISIOLO-BUFFALO SPRINGS GAME RESERVE

Isiolo